The Jeremia

About the Author

Derek Frank orignially trained as an engineer, which led to a commercial career, and then to ordination into the Church of England. He has ministered on the staff of St Thomas', Crookes, in Sheffield, England and is presently chaplain of All Saints',Vevey with St Peter's, Château-d'Oex, Switzerland

By the same Author

Tough Questions About Healing (Highland Books 1994) which addresses the issues raised by prayer for healing which is not immediately answered.

The Jeremiah Diagnosis

Derek Frank

Highland Books

First published in 2000 by Highland Books, Two High Pines, Knoll Road, Godalming, Surrey, GU7 2EP.

Copyright © 2000 Derek Frank

ISBN: 1 897913 51 6

Printed in Finland by WS Bookwell.

Acknowledgements

There is no shortage of writing about reformation, particularly as it affected the sixteenth century, and my reflections do not aim to add to historical scholarship. I would simply acknowlege my debt to those who have laboured to make the history of the Reformation accessible. Should I have missed any point, the fault is mine alone.

I must also acknowledge the vital role of three men, Loren Cunningham, Tom Bloomer and Darrow Miller, in encouraging me to consider what a new season of Reformation might mean for the Western Church. Their timely comments truly made the difference.

I also wish to express my gratitude to the congregation of All Saints', Vevey, Switzerland for their support; and most of all to my wife Françoise, and daughters Vanessa and Abigail for bearing with me as I did something that I vowed I would never do again!

*"Set up road signs;
put up guideposts.
Take note of the highway,
the road that you take.
Return, O Virgin Israel,
return to your towns"
— Jeremiah 31 v21*

Contents

Chapter One

What is Coming ?

"REVIVAL SWEEPS ACROSS EUROPE ...!" Imagine your feelings to see the headline, not only in the Christian press but splashed across the secular media as well. To know first hand the story of what has happened right where you live, with huge numbers who have never been to church in their lives turning to Christ. The whole neighbourhood being transformed, people who were once entirely consumed by their own interests becoming caring and compassionate, with a new light in their eyes, and all this as just one small part of what is impacting whole cities, touching everything from schools and universities to shops and factories. People, from the greatest to the least, living out their new found discipleship in a holy fear of God. A fresh spirit of hope filling the very sinews of a Europe that until recently had looked as if it was irredeemably defunct—surely this is the dream of every Christian, however unlikely it might seem in a Europe which has lost sight of both its spiritual heart and heritage. Yet if the dream were not to come true, what else could the future hold for the Western church as it moves into its third millennium?

For the last twenty or even thirty years revival in Britain, and in parts of Europe as well, has been reckoned to be just around the corner. It has been spoken of as increasingly imminent, and not only spoken of, but also prayed for, prophesied about and preached on as never before. Partly because of the continuing experience of renewal touching the lives of individuals and churches. Partly also because of the social, moral and spiritual decline that has increasingly permeated our society. So the conclusion has been drawn. If it is not to be the return of the Lord Jesus Christ in our time, then it has to be revival. Much hope has been invested in its early arrival, to reverse the forces of secularism and restore our churches and communities. But however well intentioned it may have been, my view is that this has been a misplaced hope.

During my last seven years working in Switzerland as an Anglican clergyman, I have reflected on what I saw of renewal in England, and since then in Europe. Clearly we live in remarkable times. But we must face the blunt fact that the process of renewal has not thus far led to anything near what has previously been defined as revival, nor does it look like doing so, for renewal seems to be circling on a plateau. Thank God that it continues to circle, and that it still blesses many as it goes round. Yet given the remarkable stories of revival now coming from all over the world, the conspicuous absence of similar reports from Europe is significant.

Clearly God's arm is not for twisting. The evidence is that we have not been able to manipulate Him into delivering a made-to-measure revival. Instead we are challenged to look beyond the urgency of the present moment, to consider why not? Especially given the history of the church in Europe. For God has declared that He does not forget people or places (Isaiah 44 v21). One thing we can be sure of is that He remembers how five centuries ago the gospel was grasped afresh in Britain and Europe and then taken out to the world through mission. Such that the history of the world since then has largely been centred around Europe, shaped as it was by the impact of the sixteenth century Reformation.

But neither will He have failed to notice how the influence of Europe has declined in parallel with the diminishing of the church within it, or how much of what remains is characterised by nominalism. Meaning that even where the church does appear to have some vitality, its influence rarely prevails beyond the private lives of its members. So that in the public arena there remains little other than ceremonial religion, as for a royal marriage, or the funeral of a celebrated princess, and that this, despite all its imposing pageantry and capacity to evoke nostalgia, lacks any real spiritual authority. Let alone the ability to restore the distinctive influence of Christianity into the public domain. A state of affairs most church members would consider to be a matter of regret, and some even as a relief. But there are not many who seem to recognise just how critical this is for the church, let alone for the nations of Europe in which it is set.

From the vantage point of His throne, God must see all this so much more clearly than we do, and therefore our diagnosis will inevitably be far less perceptive than His, as will be our prescription. Which is why the withholding of the much heralded revival is something we should take great note of. From our close up viewpoint a revival, however brief, can look like a very attractive proposition. But from God's greater overview, the respite it would doubtless bring may possibly appear to be rather less beneficial. For it may only serve to further delay the church in Europe from facing the devastating truth about how far short it falls of the role it once played in shaping nations; and from recognising how much it must grieve God to see its continued demise and decay. He may therefore be wantimg to say something very different from those who only take a short-term view of the Christian history of Europe.

Through the withholding of revival, God's word may be that radical surgery is the church's only hope for the future. If this were to be so, then the language of reformation is surely more appropriate than that of revival. Yet amidst all the expectation of revival, or even of the return of Jesus Christ, prediction of a new season of reformation has been remarkably absent. It is as if what happened back in the sixteenth century was rather like *1066 And All That:* an event in history that was a one-off, relevant only to its particular time; or something that can be wrapped up as a finished event, even if it does take many libraries of books to do so. There seems to be little perception of it being incomplete even within its own time-frame. Let alone that for both the church and the western world, the events of the past five hundred years have generated a completely new agenda for reformation.

This may explain why, in the broad spectrum of spiritual expectancy that we have seen in recent decades, there has been such a blind spot over the middle way, that lies in between revival – which brings a short-term burst of new zeal in the church, even spilling over into the surrounding community – and the Second Coming itself that will bring in perfect righteousness and justice when all things are made new. Yet it is a truly extensive middle ground, where the value systems of nations can be profoundly touched, leaving a legacy for generations to come. Indeed where God can use the words and actions of mere individuals to overturn even the monolithic structures of church and state.

Through the withholding of revival, it is my conviction, God is drawing attention to this neglected area of expectation. I neither wish to romanticise the events, let alone the disputes, of the sixteenth century as some would, nor to propose a wholesale return to our Puritan or Pietistic roots as others would, but simply to consider what the diagnosis and prescription of a modern-day Luther, Calvin or Zwingli might be, and what interpretation they would put on the moving of the Holy Spirit in a church that is fallen from its former glory. Especially as it compromises with a world estranged from the reformation principle of *coram Deo*—of all life being before God. A world where the church spires that once stood out from the city skylines, pointing up from all human activity to the One who is high over all, are now dwarfed by skyscrapers. A world that speaks of man's desire to raise himself yet higher.

How then would the great Reformers define the agenda of our time? Or the opportunity of our time, were it to be seized with the same tenacity that they exercised in the sixteenth century? My own reflections can obviously be only one very small part of the process that is needed. Which is why I would invite you to join me and others in it—though with a warning! For as we engage with the thinking of the Reformers, it will also be with the prophecy of Jeremiah, whose words to Baruch should not be forgotten:

> Should you then seek great things for yourself? Seek them not.
>
> (Jeremiah 45 v5)

Judging by how Jeremiah was largely ignored by his contemporaries, to engage with such a process may not be a fast track to popularity – since it involves challenging those who categorically state that God wants to send a hearty dose of revival to Britain and Europe right now. Indeed even to go as far as suggesting that those who confidently place their hopes in such a revival might be like the false prophets of Jeremiah's time, whose naive optimism was exposed by the catastrophic captivity in Babylon. Yet given that 'Babylon' may not be a bad description of the state of the western world as it starts the third millennium, I trust it is a process you might seriously consider involvement with.

For I would suggest that there is much relevance today in a key treatise of Luther's which was entitled *On the Babylonian Captivity of the Church*. In it he pictured the Catholic priesthood as holding Christendom to ransom through its control of the Mass. The proposition I invite you to evaluate is that the Protestant Church in the Europe of today is also in captivity, though a very different one from that of Luther's time, and that nothing less than a new season of reformation is needed for the church to be set free. Which is not to deny the mixed consequences the sixteenth century Reformation led to, from enormous good through to schism and war. Nor to suggest that a new season of reformation would be any less costly or mixed in its consequences. But that in it will lie potential far beyond anything a short-term revival might lead to. It is to this, I believe, that God is seeking to open our eyes.

May I then begin by taking you back to one of the focal points of the sixteenth century Reformation—to the city of Geneva. For in the story of Geneva, and the Reformer John Calvin who was so identified with it, lies timeless insight into the potential of reformation: potential such that a single generation is able to erect a signpost to the power of God's truth, straddling over both the nations and the generations. It is a story that speaks not only of past history, but also of future possibility. Particularly for the region of the world from which sprang the Reformation of the sixteenth century, and for what remains of the church within it.

Post Tenebras Lux

Despite it now being 450 years since the high water mark of the Genevan Reformation, there still remains immense blessing on the city because of what happened back then. Even today, 'Geneva' means something the world over. Most noticeably, it continues to exercise a prominence on the world stage out of all proportion to its size. It is home to the United Nations, the World Health Organisation, the World Council of Churches, and the Red Cross, founded there by Henry Dunant, whose Christian conviction was formed in a church in old Geneva. The city houses extensive numbers of other international institutions and hosts many thousands of international conferences every year. Indeed, it is the most likely place for warring nations to go to discuss terms of peace. For it was here that the Convention which defines the terms of engagement in international conflict, to which nations continue to hold each other accountable, was worked out. Yet all this in a city whose population is still less than half a million.

The Geneva of today is no accident of history. Even though it later turned its back on God, He has left the mark of His faithfulness upon this city that once was so open to His reforming power. For Geneva was not always the clean, modern, affluent city it is known as today. Prior to what happened in the sixteenth century, it was what one writer of the time described as "the stinkiest city in Europe". Not only was it dirty, but apparently it had more bars per head than any other major city of its time. It was in such an unfavourable atmosphere, that John Calvin sought to build a visible 'City of God.'

Today the streets that wind up and down the hill upon which the old city of Geneva is built are picturesque and character-filled. Though now they are little more than a relic of where Calvin sought to establish the kingdom of God, many of those buildings witnessed the impact of the Reformation message. It was for everybody and every area of life. Not just for Sunday, or for a private quiet time, or for an occasional mid-week meeting, but for the whole of life. There was no division between the sacred and the secular. It was all one continuum. Such was the impact of Calvin's daily preaching that at 4.00 pm the bells would ring, and the shops would close, so that everyone might go to church. The effect on the community was profound, as were the repercussions on the neighbouring cities and countries. What Calvin established there was to last for a century or more in direct terms, before the Enlightenment began to progressively erode it. Though, at least, indirectly, its effects on western society continue to this day.

Geneva had always been a crossing place, from the countries of the north through to the Mediterranean via the Swiss plateau, from France to Italy through the *cols* of the western Jura mountains, and across the Rhone by the only bridge that existed in ancient times between the Lake and the town of Lyons. However, by the second half of the 15th century, it had suffered a century of economic depression, aggravated by wars, plague and food shortages that hit the region time and time again. It had found itself caught between the determination of the Duke of Savoy to seize the town, and the similar endeavours of the communities in Fribourg and Berne. It was an uncomfortable position situated on the borders of France, Savoy and Switzerland. What the Genevans had to learn was how to maintain a balancing act that kept it from being subservient to any greater power. So it discovered how to live 'in the middle', a skill which was to be so valuable in the years to come.

In 1535, under the influence of Guillaume Farel, Geneva broke free from its allegiance to the Duke of Savoy. By decree of the city council, and under the preaching of Farel, it had formally become a Protestant city. The Catholic clergy had left, and many citizens had no desire to see them replaced by another faith. Even so, in May, 1536 those who had the right to vote decided to "live henceforth according to the holy Law of the Gospel and the Word of God, and to abolish all papal abuses." They also decided to create free public education in Geneva, and to ensure that the children of the poor were fed as well as taught. In reality, the actual work of reform had scarcely begun. Yet it was just sufficient to enable what was being prepared by God to be received, albeit rather uncomfortably.

Simultaneously in 1536, John Calvin left Paris to avoid the persecution of the Protestants. He first moved to Strasbourg, where in God's providence, he met Martin Bucer, one of the great scholars of the Reformation, who was later to play the critical role in getting him back to Geneva. When Calvin was born in 1509, Luther was already lecturing at the University of Revert. Initially Calvin was destined for a career in the church. At sixteen he was sent to the Collge Montaigu, of great repute, but noted also for its harsh, medieval methods. The principal opposed the new Reformation ideas that were spreading from Germany, yet Calvin was still introduced to the writings of the church Fathers, and particularly of St. Augustine, who later so strongly influenced his thinking. Under the impression that a career in law would yield greater returns than one in the church, he was sent to the university of Orleans, where he received his doctorate in 1533.

When, around that time, Calvin encountered the teachings of Luther, he experienced a sudden conversion experience. He had inherited an immovable will from his father, which was to stand him in good stead in later years in Geneva. Yet as a new convert he commented "God subdued and brought my heart to docility. It was more hardened against such matters than was to be expected in such a young man." Greatly changed, he broke with Roman Catholicism, and became a refugee.

In the same year he published the first edition of his *Institutes of the Christian Religion*, which he continued revising up to 1559. Though initially just six brief chapters, it constituted the first systematic exposition of Reformed teaching, since described as "the masterpiece of Protestant theology." Based on the Apostles' Creed, it showed how the Reformers were leading believers back to the beliefs and practices of the Early Church. When it became a best seller, the timid young scholar became known as an up-and-coming proponent of the Reformation. So much so, that when Farel heard that Calvin was travelling through Geneva, he sought him out with the greatest urgency. Farel implored him to stay and assist in completing the newly won commitment to Reformation.

Farel recognised both the need and the opportunity of the moment. The city had, in effect, become lawless. Despite the corruption of the Roman Catholic church, it had previously provided the rule of law. When the Bishop was eventually expelled, it left the city free, but without a legal system. The declaration of the Genevans might seem to have created a reformed church, but in fact, all it did was to create a reform-minded vacuum.[1] To reject Catholicism was one thing, but to build a new system of church government and order was another. Chaos was a distinct possibility. Something needed to happen, and Farel had no doubt been praying hard.

At the time, Calvin was travelling from Paris to Strasbourg, where he had hoped to settle down to his long-desired life of leisure and study. However, troop movements forced him to take a more southerly route obliging him to go through Geneva. His impression of the city was such that he decided to stay one night only. He was therefore doubly shocked at Farel's proposal. He protested that he was ill-suited for the task, and could better edify the church by his quiet study and writing. Farel, however, was undaunted by such a meagre excuse.

One account relates how, with flashing eyes and formidable red beard, Farel thundered down the curse of God upon Calvin in words he could never forget. Calvin described the "fearsome adjuration" in these terms: "At this point Farel (burning with a wondrous zeal to advance the gospel), suddenly set all his efforts at keeping me. After having heard that I was determined to pursue my own private studies—when he realised he would get nowhere by pleas—he came to the point of a curse: that it would please God to curse my leisure and the quiet for my studies that I was seeking, if in such a grave emergency I should withdraw and refuse to give aid and help. This word so overwhelmed me that I hesitated from the journey I had undertaken."[2]

From that moment, Calvin was linked to Geneva. Through the sovereignty of God, the great Reformer had been led to the city so long at the crossroads of Europe. He was to shape, and be shaped, by Geneva. Its transformation from a place where nude dancing had taken place in the streets to the definitive city of morality had huge international consequences. Through it the all-encompassing power of the Cross was demonstrated. It was not just for individuals—it was for cities, and therefore for nations as well. To this day, there is perhaps no other place in the world that has been so seen as a moral city. Neither what happened subsequently through the Enlightenment's impact on this 'City of God,' nor the reality of the spiritual state of Geneva today, 450 years later, has completely eliminated the legacy of what happened at that time.

However, it did not come without great battle. Between 1536 and 1538, Calvin drew up a list of articles of faith, teaching people that they should live according to the New Testament. He proposed that church members should be excommunicated, involving loss of citizenship, if they were not prepared to live by God's word. He set up a system of control, and through the city council appointed elders whose job was to monitor people's conduct. It was not easy imposing law and order on the lawless people of Geneva, especially as a foreigner. Many opposed Calvin strongly. Disputes in the town resulted, and in April 1538 both Calvin and Farel left the town, though not without first ex-communicating everybody!

Calvin then went to Strasbourg, where he had been heading before being, as it were, waylaid by Farel. Three formative years followed there for him. He became pastor to a congregation of French refugees. He taught and he wrote, revising the Institutes and producing his commentary on Romans. He acted as a church statesman working for Christian unity, and he also got married. Each experience was preparation for what was to come for in September 1541 the Genevans implored him to return, things having gone from bad to worse. They now wanted not just religious peace but to consolidate the work of Reformation there. Calvin was reluctant to leave Strasbourg to return to that "dangerous gulf and whirlpool ... that cross on which I had to perish daily a thousand times over." But yet again he was threatened into doing what by natural inclination he would not have done. This time by Martin Bucer who suggested that if he did not resume his ministry in Geneva, Calvin would be acting just like Jonah who tried to run away from God.

As he returned to preach, the Genevans anticipated a triumphalist lambasting of those who had caused Farel and him to leave. Instead, he simply picked up the exposition of the very chapter and verse he had reached at the time of his expulsion. Thereby he gave the clearest signal of his commitment to a continuing ministry. It was to mark the start of his attempt to make Geneva into a 'City of God,' modelled on the New Testament. He presented to the city council a detailed revision of the city laws, and a plan for the government of the church. He also set about attaining his aim of a mature church by preaching daily. The result was that in 1556 the Scottish Reformer, John Knox, described Geneva as "the most perfect school of Christ that was ever on earth since the days of the apostles."

It was built on the pure preaching of God's word, faithful celebration of the sacraments, and firm enforcement of discipline involving regular examination of the faith and morals of ministers and congregation. Some objected that Calvin's austere discipline spoilt all the fun. His tribunals were certainly mocked, when things as minor as too much noise in the street could be judged. Yet the punishment of adultery by death rapidly impacted the relaxed morals of the day, and a new emphasis on the sanctity of marriage was quickly established. Some said his courts led to Pharisaism and hypocrisy, imposing an unbearable tyranny. But in just one generation, the previously dysfunctional family life of the city was transformed. Responsibility and accountability were proclaimed, prompting people to work diligently, and prosperity resulted. Geneva also became international, with the arrival of the moral and religious elite of Europe. The poor and the sick were helped, and respect for the teaching of children was upheld, for in them lay the future. As Calvin stood against godlessness, the spiritual history of Geneva was purged. The people of the day were completely changed, and the city was changed for generations to come.

Geneva also became one of the principle places of refuge for Protestants persecuted for their religion. When Protestantism was declared illegal in France, both individuals and cities were required to declare allegiance to the Catholic church. The only alternatives were for people to leave, or face martyrdom. Many came to Geneva as an open city. So it was that in the ten years from 1550, 5,000 refugees were welcomed to a town that previously had only 10,000 inhabitants.

The motto Calvin gave to the city was *Post Tenebras Lux*, meaning 'After the Darkness, Light.' When he died in 1564, Geneva, though still developing, was already influencing cities far away. However, the context in which this had come about should not be missed. It was one of intense struggle. He wrote:

> Satan ... a thousand times a day draws us away from the right course.

> I say nothing of fire and sword and exiles and all the furious attacks of our enemies. I say nothing of slanders and other such vexations. How many things there are within us that are far worse! Ambitious men openly attack us, Epicureans and Lucianists mock us, impudent men insult us, hypocrites rage against us, those who are wise after the flesh do us harm, and we are harassed in many different ways on every side. The only remedy for all these difficulties is to look forward to Christ's appearing and always to put our trust in it.

Evidently in Calvin's view, the fullness of Reformation would only come as the final, eschatological act of God. That, though, did not prevent him from pressing on as far as he could with a practical outworking of it for the situation in which he lived. The far-reaching consequences of what happened as a result should surely challenge us to reflect on what God could similarly do in our generation or the next—for the need to see some new reformation light in Europe after the darkness of the twentieth century is immense.

Signs of the times

The story of Geneva, and all that arose out of what happened from its example, demonstrates the potential of reformation. It shows how it is possible, not only for cities, but also for nations to be reformed out of all recognition. Just the residual blessing that remains on Geneva today is sufficient to draw attention to this reality. But, for reformation to happen, there needs to be sufficient conjunction of circumstance. Had it not been for Calvin's tenacious mentality, or his willingness to engage in severe spiritual battle, let alone his extraordinary range of gifts, as theologian, lawyer and organiser, it may never have taken place. But had it not also been for Farel's and Bucer's threats, Calvin may never have been in Geneva at all. Nor might he have even arrived there in the first place had it not been for the military activity that prompted him to change route on the way to Strasbourg. Indeed, had there not been the particular flow of events that led the Genevans to their declaration of May, 1536, there may have been neither the need nor the opportunity for Calvin in Geneva.

In fact it had taken a much greater set of circumstances to set up the milieu of the Reformation. For the reason why the Reformation took place in the sixteenth century, rather than in the two or three preceding centuries was not because of an earlier lack of fervent religious devotion.[3] Certainly the late medieval church had become increasingly corrupt as each century went by, but the desire and demands for reformation had been expressed for centuries. The greater religious scene had not been a complete desert of neglect and abuse, for there had been abundant signs of lively religious activity at numerous levels for many years. But of themselves, they were inadequate to shake the control of the church and precipitate a reformation. That required the conjunction of two other developments, neither of which was religious in itself.

The first was the emergence of the Renaissance. Originally only a term in the history of art, it came to represent a period of cultural flourishing which swept through Italy and then Northern Europe from the fourteenth to the sixteenth centuries. Its scholars were consciously living a 're-birth' of classical learning which had separated the fall of Rome in the fifth century from their own period. Though certain classical authors had been known through the Middle Ages, the study of Greek had been almost unknown in Western Europe before 1400. However, when in 1453 Constantinople was sacked by the Turks, its classical scholars fled westwards, taking their books with them. With the arrival of both Greek manuscripts and academics who could read them, came two things. One was the opening up of the rational ways of Greek thinking, which was to have such great upside and also such great downside for the Reformation. The other was the technique it brought of going back to the original text, to ask what it originally meant. It was this which was to be so critical in Luther's seminal discovery that the Greek word *dikaios*, 'just,' contained two meanings, 'justice' (actually being just) and 'justification' (being counted as just).

An equally significant piece of timing was the invention of the printing press. Johann Gutenberg's pioneering of moveable metal type was to transform the world of printing. It was to be a milestone in the history of communication. Though the art of printing from hand-cut wooden blocks dated back to the fifth century AD, it was not until around 1445 that Europe was to develop the 'art of artificial writing' as it was called. The first book known to have been printed in the Christian world came in 1446. Significantly, it was the Bible. Subsequently, it was the printing of the voluminous writings of Luther, Calvin and the other Reformers that so energised the spread of the Reformation.

With this also came the pamphlet, the forerunner of the newspaper. Given our familiarity with news, it is hard to imagine what it was like to depend mainly on the only forms of public announcement which then existed—the town crier, and the sermon. Otherwise, people depended on letters, word of mouth and news brought by travellers. Pamphlets, which did not have to toe the official line, could be printed anywhere, and had the potential not only to carry news, but also to be subversive. With their advent, it then became possible to appeal to public opinion on a scale undreamed of before, by-passing the authorities and hierarchies. The early spread of the Reformation hinged greatly on what the printing press made possible.

Thus it was that the breakthrough in studies of language, and the technology of printing, joined with the long-standing demands for reformation to result in it happening in the sixteenth century. From a human perspective, it could simply be said that this was when the long-overdue coincidence eventually happened. But from a spiritual perspective, it can also be said that this was the appointed time for the 'God-incidence' to take place. For with the eye of faith it is not hard to see the sovereign hand of God throughout the story of the sixteenth century Reformation, bringing together many different people and circumstances. It is therefore both history and His story. Which is not altogether surprising, given that scripture tells us that amidst the apparently free-running events of this world, God has His appointed times. The greatest of all works of reformation, when Christ died for the ungodly, happened "at just the right time" (Romans 5 v6). It was "when the time had fully come" (Galatians 4 v4), that resulted in the "testimony given in its proper time" (1 Timothy 2 v6) "at His appointed season" (Titus 1 v3). Given the present situation of the western church and the nations in which it is set, this leads to the most vital question. Is there sufficient conjunction in the present signs of the times to suggest that this could be another of those God-appointed times for a new season of reformation?

We have already considered the prevailing, unfulfilled sense of expectancy of revival that in itself suggests the need for another explanation, for which other indications do exist. The most obvious is that we are again at the point of unparalleled breakthrough in the ability to communicate. All too quickly we lose sight of just how recent in the time frame of history is the computer revolution. Only twenty years ago, personal calculators were just coming in. Personal computers were still one jump ahead, and the world-wide web, the idea of which happened to originate in Geneva, was unheard of. Nowadays the average schoolchild of the western world considers them a completely normal part of life. But the quantum jump of the last few years in the ability to communicate has been so great, it has only been paralleled twice before in the last two thousand years.

The last time when such a sudden jump was achieved was with the invention of the printing press, and as we have already considered, it was this that so facilitated the sixteenth century Reformation. The previous time was about fifteen hundred years earlier, with the arrival of the *Pax Romana*, the Roman peace. Amongst other things, it established safe travel over great distances along superbly engineered roads, and with that, the scope for previously unparalleled communication. It was this that enabled news of the greatest reformation of all to spread so rapidly, as the gospel of salvation was taken from place to place, eventually leading to the official conversion of the Roman Empire within three centuries. Indeed Pentecost itself was exemplified by the gift of a previously-unknown means of communication. So if the arrival of the world-wide web proves to be as significant as that of the printing press and of Roman roads, the release of a new season of reformation might not be so improbable.

Another sign of the times is that seasons of reformation seem to have their best opportunity as historical eras come to an end. One of the reasons why the sixteenth century Reformation, which was basically a theological matter, had the impact it did was because it appealed to all sorts of people, of all classes and conditions. It not only answered the religious question of "How can I be right with God—and be sure of it?" but it went so much further still. For it enabled a breaking out of the prevailing system of feudalism, with all its social and economic constraints, into a new understanding of life.

At the start of the twenty-first century, modernism—that last expression of the rationalist thinking of the Enlightenment that followed the sixteenth century Reformation—is reaching the end of its life. Sociologists are describing what is coming next to the western world as post-modernism, because thus far it can only really be defined by what it is not. At the same time, in the global perspective, though communism has collapsed, there is a deep suspicion that this does not prove capitalism to be right. Indeed, it too could soon collapse. Thus there is a sense of vacuum, if not of the coming to the end of another era of history, that could further enhance the opportunity of a new season of reformation.

Of course the conjunction of these circumstances can simply be dismissed as conjecture. Yet what if it were not to be, and was actually pointing to a once-every-five-hundred-years possibility? How will we in the church in Britain, Europe, or indeed anywhere in the western world, respond as it unfolds? For there can be no reformation of society unless the church is first willing to be reformed itself. *Ecclesia semper reformanda*—the church always in need of reform—applies to any period. But whereas the vision of revival has a whiff of triumphalism to it, that of reformation does not. Given the possibility of the times we are in, this may mean the church being shaken to the core as it is once again taken back to the basics of the Christian message. How much the truth of what this would mean is recognised, let alone responded to, is the determining question.

Over two thousand years before the time of Calvin, the Old Testament prophet Jeremiah had witnessed Josiah's bold attempt at reform, which seemed to take hold, and then was lost. Through him God spoke these words:

> Stand at the gate of the Lord's house, and there proclaim this message:

> Hear the word of the Lord, all you people of Judah who come through these gates to worship the Lord. This is what the Lord Almighty, the God of Israel, says: "Reform your ways and your actions, and I will let you live in this place. Do not trust in deceptive words and say, 'This is the temple of the Lord, the temple of the Lord, the temple of the Lord!'

> "If you really change your ways and your actions and deal with each other justly, if you do not oppress the alien, the fatherless or the widow and do not shed innocent blood in this place, and if you do not follow other gods to your own harm, then I will let you live in this place, in the land I gave to your forefathers for ever. But look, you are trusting in deceptive words that are worthless."

Though the circumstances were specific to the time, the prophetic challenge of Jeremiah still echoes across history. For in the western church, we too may be under a delusion, if not a deception, about our condition. Even if we physically live where the great Reformers once lived, the reality is that we no longer do so spiritually. We do not see the basic message of the gospel changing the course of the nations, let alone of history itself, though we know of its power to do so. Instead, when the need for the healing of society is so deep, to quote another phrase of Jeremiah, we only seem to be healing the wounds of the people "lightly" (Jeremiah 6 v14 RSV).

High up in the Swiss Alps, it is said that there is a very special ridge. When the snow on it melts, depending on which way it tilts, the water from it can go in one of two directions. It can flow to the north, winding its way through a series of streams until it reaches the River Rhine, and from there it flows northwards to the chilly waters of the North Sea. But if the same melt water goes the other way, it can instead flow through another series of streams, and eventually reach the River Rhone. From there it flows southwards, to the warm waters of the Mediterranean. Two very different destinations can be reached from the same starting point. Which may also apply to the great volume of spiritual melt water that will flow from the western church, if it continues its present rate of melt down through the next generation.

The signs of our times suggest that there exists the rare opportunity for it to flow in the direction of reformation, with historic consequence. After the darkness of the twentieth century it could bring new light. But the message of scripture is that unless the church first comes out of its grand delusion,

God could equally permit the flow to be in the opposite direction. Such that the church and the nations it serves, could go into spiritual decimation. At our point in history, either is possible. And which becomes more probable may depend on nothing more than the tilt that we of this generation give to the choices we make.

Chapter Two

Different Types of Fruit

SUDDEN CHANGE IS NOT what the established church of today is well known for. In a world where constant change seems to be the only unchanging fact, this implies both strength and weakness. On the one hand, it offers reassurance that there are some eternal verities that even the greatest changes of this world can never alter. But on the other, it suggests that the church is increasingly irrelevant. That it needs to get up to date, and back in touch with where the action truly is. This, though, is not the reason why the western church may now be facing a season of change unparalleled in the past five hundred years. For the origins of why it may be about to go one of two ways—into reformation, or into decimation—are much longer term. Origins that are best illuminated by looking beyond the differences between the present western church and its late-medieval ancestor, to the points of similarity.

History makes no secret of how corrupt and riddled with abuses the late medieval church was. The Papacy and all those in high office were indistinguishable from their secular counterparts, living a life of great luxury with little sense of responsibility for their calling. Bishops saw nothing wrong with accumulating several dioceses and never visiting them, and clergy often had only the scarcest knowledge of theology. The laity were restricted to the nave of the church, whilst the clergy celebrated services in the chancel in Latin, hidden behind a massive rood screen. Consequently even the most faithful had only the vaguest notion of true religion which meant that enormous scope abounded for externalised religion, not to mention superstition, witchcraft, magic and much other hocus-pocus.

But it was not that there was no heart for salvation in the people. The primary question for many genuinely was "how can I get right with God?" For this, the church offered its all-embracing answer, or at least its all-embracing system. It began with the sacrament of penance. The believer confessed to the priest, who prescribed what the sinner had to do to make amends. The penance might be quite minimal, such as reciting some prayers, going on a fast, or making a gift. However, it could involve a pilgrimage, and for those with the means, it could go as far as building a chapel or even a cathedral. Having completed the penance, or at least undertaken to, the sinner could be absolved by the priest, and the slate wiped clean. But only until the next time and with no guarantee about the ultimate question of all. Not just how death was to be faced, but moreover, how the almighty Judge was to be faced.

Hence the place of another sacrament. Extreme unction was the final act of confession and forgiveness, at the point of death. Herein was further protection, unless death was unexpectedly sudden. Even then, there was one more stage in the system—purgatory. The prospect of cleansing fire was terrifying, given the suffering already endured by so many in their short, brutish, plague-ridden lives. Yet, after cleansing, one's place could then be taken in heaven. Furthermore, prayers and masses could be said for the dead in order to reduce their time in purgatory. Most significantly, indulgences for the dead could not only be obtained by spiritual acts, but ultimately could also be purchased. Hence the practice which eventually became so lucrative to the church until the day when Luther decided the gravy train had to stop.

However, despite the comprehensiveness of the system, there was no final assurance in it, even for the most sincere. But in the absence of any alternative, it was all the people had. They were absolutely dependent on the system, and on the purveyor of it—the priest. He alone could pronounce the words of absolution—*ego absolvo te*. Only he had the power to change bread and wine into the body and blood of Christ. Only he could minister the sacraments of baptism and extreme unction. Given that a baby who had not been baptised did not go to heaven, the priest and the church held great power. By reinforcing the prospect of hell and purgatory, they drove people to the sacraments of the church, and held them in great bondage as they did so.

Looking back on the situation of the sixteenth century, it is not too hard for us to see through it all. From both scripture, and the heart-centred experience of assurance, we know what is the power of the gospel. We understand and experience salvation as pure gift, which no amount of good works can ever achieve (Ephesians 2 v8-9). Furthermore that our doing of good works is no more than gratitude for the fact that we are going to heaven. Thus we do them because we are going there, not in order to get there. With this perspective, it is not difficult to see how erroneous was the place of the priest in the church of the sixteenth century, let alone how rife with hypocrisy was the institution of the church, or how off course was its theology. Yet for those of the time, it was rather less easy to discern exactly what was wrong.

There was the persistent suspicion that things were far from right, and that reform was long overdue. But what exactly the reform was that was needed, let alone how it was to be implemented, was extremely hard to deduce. There was a thick cloud of delusion, if not deception, that enveloped even the most sincere of believers. To see sufficiently far through it to expose where the church had gone wrong, and why its authority had to be challenged, required a sort of supernatural night vision that very few seemed to have. But beyond that lay the most insuperable question of all: just how could such a massive power structure as the church ever be confronted? The pressure to acquiesce was therefore enormous.

At the start of the third millennium, it is not difficult to distinguish between the western church of today and the late-medieval church as it was half-way through the second millennium. The challenge however is to see beyond the distinctions to the similarities. For we too have a long-standing sense that things are far from right. We hear of the amazing growth of the church in other parts of the world through this last century, whilst to quote the Archbishop of Canterbury speaking to the 1998 World Council of Churches Assembly in Zimbabwe, parts of the western church are "bleeding to death." Few in Britain and Europe really believe that the church we are a part of is as good as it gets. Yet not only we, but apparently our senior leaders also, have great difficulty in putting our finger on what exactly is wrong, let alone to work out how things could ever be changed. Meanwhile the greater proportion of the residual membership of the western church remains in a relatively convenient and compliant acquiescence.

Such acquiescence is therefore not without parallel to that which existed in the church of the Middle Ages, prior to the sixteenth century Reformation. Though the reality is that every generation of the church has the potential to acquiesce; as it does so, it comes first under delusion, and then under deception, thereby giving Satan the opportunity to move it toward destruction. Nose up to the present situation, it is hard to assess just how close the western church may be to that point right now. But in a few hundred years' time, it is not unlikely that the compliant acceptance of the present failings of the western church may be seen as vastly more blatant than is presently recognised. Indeed our level of delusion about today's 'temple of the Lord' may be far beyond anything we yet realise.

The story of what happened in Geneva a century after the era of Calvin is proof positive of what can happen. For by the end of the eighteenth century, it was possible to study in Calvin's Academy without opening a Bible except for the need to read a few Psalms when Hebrew was being studied. Indeed when Voltaire went to Geneva, he was quoted as saying, "I met with the pastors, but there was not a Christian amongst them." Such was the impact on Geneva of imbibing the thinking of the Enlightenment. This had prompted a move away from revealed religion, to make room for the place for reason, which it was believed offered the absolute basis for achieving greater wisdom. Amongst its many effects was the reduction of the person of Jesus Christ to simply a great moral leader and teacher, and the declaration that the doctrine of a saving sacrifice on the cross for all mankind was a superstition. Almost unimaginable in the very seat of the one who had organised Reformed Protestantism. Yet that is precisely what happened. Such is the power of

Satan to throw a cloak of delusion and deception over an unsuspecting church, unless it is extremely perceptive about what is happening to it.

The same pattern is to be found in many places in the history of God's people. From the letters to the seven churches in Revelation chapters two and three, we see how quickly delusion set into the early church. Probably dating from within the first century AD, we find that most of the churches written to were already deluded, if not deceived, about their true condition. Worse still, that they lacked any real awareness of where the slippery slope they were on might lead to. Typical are the words to the church in Ephesus "You have forsaken your first love" (Revelation 2 v4). This stinging rebuke was addressed to the very church to which Paul had declared that salvation was by grace, through faith and not of works. The diagnosis though was simple. Its initial passion for the Lord had not been regenerated. Some points of commendation remained, but, given where it had reached, removal of its lampstand was already a distinct possibility. And without the Light, the cloud of darkness would quickly descend.

Similarly, it was also only a relatively short number of years after King Josiah's courageous attempt at reformation, that Jeremiah had to challenge God's people about trusting in deceptive words that were worthless. Despite coming to the throne at a mere eight years of age Josiah had begun to seek God. It was a lonely quest, for he had many foes and very few allies. Yet, when just twenty, he courageously began to purge the religiosity of his day. He broke down the altars of the Baals, and the graven and molten images were broken into pieces, and then pulverised into powder.

When still only twenty-six, he began to restore the temple. This God mightily honoured. For in the process of the repair work, in 622 BC, the Book of the Law was rediscovered. Most likely it contained much of what we now know as Deuteronomy. As it was read to him, Josiah was struck with profound contrition and remorse. Such was the experience of 'back to the text' that in grief for his own sins, and those of the nation, he tore his official robes. Then he began to put together further reforms. He renewed the covenant to follow the Lord and keep his commands, and he led the people in pledging themselves to it. He broke down yet more shrines and altars. He re-instated the lapsed celebration of the Passover. Finally, he got rid of the mediums and spiritists, the idols and all other detestable things seen in Judah and Jerusalem.

It was a dramatic attempt at reformation, not dissimilar in style to what Calvin had sought to do in Geneva. But tragically, in only twelve years following his death in battle aged thirty-nine, under four different kings, Judah again turned away from God. Repentance in the time of Josiah had evidently only been shallow and short-lived, and the roots of Judah's propensity for sin had evidently not been truly touched. The consequence was that in 597 BC, much of Judah was taken captive into Babylon. One day soon afterwards, when Jeremiah was standing in front of the Temple, he saw two baskets of figs. The first contained very good figs, the early-ripening variety, that were valued as a delicacy. The second contrasted sharply, for it contained rotten figs. When the Lord asked Jeremiah "What do you see?" Jeremiah replied,

> Figs. The good ones are very good, but the poor ones are so bad that they cannot be eaten.
>
> (Jeremiah 24 v3)

For around twenty-five years Jeremiah had been prophesying about the spiritual condition of Judah. Now, as he looked at these two baskets of figs, he could see they represented the two aspects of the nation. There had been both good produce and bad produce. Yet God's interpretation of the vision might not have been what he expected.

> Like these good figs, I regard as good the exiles from Judah, whom I sent away from this place to the land of the Babylonians. My eyes will watch over them for their good, and I will bring them back to this land. I will build them up and not tear them down: I will plant them and not uproot them. I will give them a heart to know me, that I am the Lord. They will be my people, and I will be their God, for they will return to me with all their heart.
>
> (Jeremiah 24 v5-7)

It was not those who had been sent into exile that were the bad figs. They were the good ones. It was the ones who were left behind that were the bad figs. They had been left to become

> a reproach and a byword, an object of ridicule and of cursing.
>
> (Jeremiah 24 v9)

As we compare the state of the church in the western world with what is going on in the other parts of the world, we can shrug our shoulders and conclude "that's just how it is." We can simply accept that most of what we know of God's power only comes from the distance of either history or geography. Or alternatively we can allow Jeremiah's picture of the two baskets of figs to speak into the situation we find ourselves in. Because if God's ways are unchanging, we may anticipate that He will work with the church of today in exactly the same way as He worked with Judah and Geneva. Just because an historic Reformation happened in a certain place, and in its season produced much good fruit, that place is not guaranteed to remain permanently reformed, or its fruit to remain. Indeed, if a subsequent generation rejects what God has done, God's pattern is to move the good fruit out into exile, and to watch over it there, rather than leave it in the place that has rejected Him. Furthermore, He will even allow what is left behind to be exposed for what it truly is.

If history is "the past and the present having a conversation about the future", then where the good fruit from the past Reformation is presently to be found should challenge the western church deeply. But, if the reality and the reason for it indicated by scripture is ignored, then the western church only has itself to blame for what may happen. For the warning of scripture is clear. Equally however, is the promise of scripture. If the western church were to acknowledge its condition, and repent, then this is what God says:

> If you repent, I will restore you that you may serve me;
> if you utter worthy, not worthless, words, you will be
> my spokesman.
>
> (Jeremiah 15 v19)

Decimation of a corrupt church is not automatically the consequence. It can be averted, and indeed the situation which brought it to that possibility can even be harnessed for good, given the appropriate repentance. For restoration, if not reformation, is always in God's heart. Which means that despite the condition the western church has fallen into, God could once more speak through it in order to impact the nations of the world. And the distinctive privilege of the western church is to have already in its ancestry the hands-on experience of reformation, beyond anything that it might have ever thought or imagined at the time. If something can happen once, it can happen again, depending, that is, on where it chooses to stand. For which reason we now turn to Martin Luther, and what led to his famous words, "Here I stand, I can do no other."

The Revelation of the Reformation

Luther was born in 1483 into a world dominated by superstition, fear of evil spirits, purgatory and eternal damnation—though still with some hope of heaven for those who did good. He was brought up as a good Catholic, though for him the mass was no more than a required ritual. He was destined to become a lawyer until, aged twenty-two, the course of his life, and of a great deal else, was altered by a bolt of lightning. Profoundly shocked by the narrowness of his escape he vowed to become a monk. Then followed a year of study that led to his becoming a priest. Unbeknown to him however, it was also to lead to another moment of terror that was to be a further crucial turning point for him. This time it was his first mass, when he found himself shrinking from what he was doing. How could he, the sinner that he was, hold in his hands the very body and blood of Christ, and not incur the wrath of the living God? And so began his struggle for an answer no-one but God could give him.

In 1510-11 Luther went to Rome, yet it was neither her former glories nor her developing splendour that were to impact him. He was deeply shocked by the irreverence of the Italian clergy, but worse still he was left in even greater doubt about the power of works or indulgences to save any soul, let alone his own. His companion described one of their experiences like this:

Today we gazed on the Veronica—the holy impression left by our Saviour's face on the cloth St. Veronica presented to him to wipe his brow, bowed under the weight of the cross. We had looked forward to this sight for days; for seven thousand years of indulgence from penance are attached to it. But when the moment came, Brother Martin and I could see nothing but a black board hung with a cloth, before which another cloth was held. In a few minutes this was withdrawn, and the great moment was over, the glimpse of the sacred thing on which hung the fate of seven thousand years![1]

Amongst many other rituals, Luther ascended on his knees the Santa Scala — the Holy Staircase — that was once supposed to be part of Pilate's house, but which he was told had been miraculously transported from Jerusalem to Rome. On each step, already worn into hollows by the knees of penitents and pilgrims, he recited the Lord's prayer. For this act of devotion was attached an indulgence from purgatory of a thousand years. Yet halfway up he suddenly stood upright, having thought he had heard a voice from heaven saying "the just shall live by faith." He shuddered, ashamed at seeing what a depth superstition had plunged him. It is said he fled far from the scene.[2]

It was a very downcast Luther who returned home, doubting that all his works were of any avail. In 1511 he was sent to the newly founded University of Wittenberg, where Frederick the Wise had amassed a huge collection of relics, to pay for the development of the town and the university. By viewing them on the Eve of All Saints', October 31st, and making the appropriate confession, indulgences from purgatory of 1,443 years could be obtained. Luther instead placed his hope in confession, but despite constant, and exceedingly extended times of confession, his soul remained in turmoil, for fear of having forgotten something. Out of this however came a critical realisation. Though confession could deal with sins, if they could all be remembered, it still could not deal with his basic condition. His problem was not so much with his own sins, as with sin in general. What needed to be dealt with was the bottom line fact of all human nature—that man is basically corrupt.

As the newly appointed Professor of Theology, he lectured extensively. In the process of this he applied the newly acquired study principle of 'back to the text.' What, in the original, did scripture really mean? In 1513, it all came to a head for him. In preparing a lecture on the Psalms, he read "Deliver me in your righteousness" (Psalm 31 v1). Whereas before he had understood righteousness to be the punishment of a holy God towards sinful man, he began to see it differently. Instead of this idea that caused him so much unease, Luther began to reflect on Romans 1 v17, and on its message that "righteousness is, from first to last, by faith." It was by faith that man was made right with God, rather than by works. Righteousness was therefore not achieved by a process of punishment. Instead, it was in God's nature to show mercy and forgiveness, that we might be declared righteous despite what we are in our nature. Then came the breakthrough. His testimony was this.

> Night and day I pondered until I grasped the truth that the righteousness of God is that righteousness whereby, through grace and sheer mercy, He justifies us by faith. Thereupon, I felt myself to be reborn and to have gone through open doors into paradise. The whole scripture took on a new meaning, and whereas before the 'righteousness of God' had filled me with hate, now it became to me inexpressibly sweet in greater love. This passage in Paul became to me a gateway to heaven.

Luther had re-discovered the good fruit of the gospel that had been driven into exile for a thousand years or more. Instead of bondage to the sacraments that left a gaping void in the vital matter of assurance, here at long, long last was both freedom and assurance *without* the necessity of a *priest* as an intermediary.

It was, however, a further four years before Luther openly challenged the false doctrines and practices of the church, which had for so long been accepted as it was. This was triggered by the arrival of the Pope's emissary, Johann Tetzel, to a town close to Wittenberg, as Frederick did not welcome too much local competition with his own collection of relics. However, what Tetzel had on offer was a very special promotion. Absolution of all sins, plus an indulgence for the souls of dead relatives who would straight away be released into heaven. He even had his own marketing jingle:

> As soon as the coin in the coffer rings,
> the soul from purgatory springs.

Tetzel was seeking to raise money through the sale of such indulgences for the rebuilding of St. Peter's in Rome. But though he did not realise it at the time, he was precipitating the building of another church—one which was to be in exile from Rome.

Luther was deeply grieved that the people were being so cruelly fleeced. They were paying on a clearly defined scale for exactly nothing at all. The time had come to act. It was not that he set out to reform the church, let alone the world. But the time had come to confront the practice of selling indulgences. It was false. It was not what scripture said. The people were being utterly misled, and the institution which was doing so had to be challenged. The only way to do so was by public debate. So very deliberately, on October 31st, 1517, Luther drew up his 95 Theses, and posted them on the door of the Castle Church in Wittenberg.

His argument was quite clear. Although an ecclesiastical indulgence may remit a penalty imposed by the church, it could not bring about the release of a soul from purgatory. He declared: "Those who assert that a soul straight away flies out of purgatory as the coin tinkles in the collection box are preaching an invention of man." His aim was to expose the church's preoccupation with material treasures, rather than with its true wealth, the gospel. Though attacking indulgences and papal misrule, Luther did not seek to attack the church in its essence. His aim was simply to sift the good fruit from the bad. So he posted his Theses in Latin, which was the language of the clergy, but not of the people, whom he did not want to draw into the debate. The only other thing he did was to send a copy to Archbishop Albert of Mainz to demand a debate. However, the effect of doing so was more than sufficient. For it was rather like the removal of a vital structural component in a multi-storey building. A progressive, catastrophic collapse resulted.

Though Luther had not intended his Theses for circulation, scholars quickly translated them into German and had them printed. With the discontent that had long been growing beneath the surface of the 16th century church, the news of them spread like wildfire. Within weeks, every university and religious centre in Europe had heard what the professor of Theology at the University of Wittenberg had propounded. Through this one action, the myth that lay behind the acquiescence of the Medieval Church was exploded. It was a consequence that the relatively obscure monk had neither expected nor intended. He had only wanted to debate the issue of indulgences, as an unbiblical practice that had grown up over centuries. Yet in the sovereign timing of God, he not only lit the blue touch paper of the sixteenth century Reformation, but soon found himself fanning its flames.

Whilst Luther never worked to a strategic plan, in the following years he nonetheless wrote prodigiously, and his books were printed and re-printed in great quantities. In doing so huge numbers of people received the revelation of the Reformation, and were mightily blessed. But Luther also alienated many. Thus it was that in 1520 the Pope issued his famous bull excommunicating Luther as a heretic, and demanding the burning of all his books. Characteristically,

Luther replied by burning the Pope's bull and writing three more books.

Eventually, he was summonsed to appear in the town of Worms, to answer questions about his teachings and writings, and was granted safe conduct to do so. The culmination of the trial before the resplendent Charles V was the requirement that he recant. It is reported that the orator said to him indignantly,

"You have not answered the questions put to you. You were not called here to call into question the decisions of councils. You are required to give a clear and precise answer. Will you, or will you not, retract?"

Upon this Luther replied without hesitation: "Since your most serene majesty and your high mightiness require from me a clear, simple and precise answer, I will give you one, and it is this: I cannot submit my faith either to the Pope, or to the councils, because it is clear as the day that they have frequently erred and contradicted each other. Unless therefore I am convinced by the testimony of Scripture, or by the clearest reasoning—unless I am persuaded by means of the passages I have quoted—and unless they thus render my conscience bound by the Word of God, I cannot and will not retract, for it is unsafe for a Christian to speak against his conscience." And then, looking round on this assembly before which he stood, and which held his life in its hands, he said "Here I stand, I can do no other; may God help me! Amen!"[3]

For Luther, there was only one authority by which good fruit could be sifted from bad, and that was the word of God. "A single layman" he once said "armed with Scripture is to be believed above the Pope or a Council without it." Here in his view was the sufficient basis of the Reformation message. Sufficient also, though Luther never intended it, for schism with the Roman church to be precipitated.

Partly due to public support, Luther was allowed to leave Worms unharmed, though a death sentence was subsequently voted for. Even so, it gave him time to escape, and he spent the following ten months in Wartburg castle, still writing furiously. Eventually he returned to Wittenburg, under the safe protection of Frederick the Wise. From there, the Reformed spirit spread to other cities. Luther pressed on with reforming the church's faith and doctrine, though still respecting some of the Catholic traditions. However, the process of Reformation had been sparked and many others poured fuel on the fire. It soon spread beyond Germany, most notably to Switzerland, under the leading of Huldrych Zwingli. And the rest, as it is said, is history.

Sola Power

Luther shunned any significant credit for what he had done. In a sermon in 1522 he said:

> I simply taught, preached, wrote God's Word; otherwise I did nothing. And then, while I slept, or drank Wittenberg beer with my Philip and my Amsdorf, the Word so greatly weakened the Papacy that never a prince or emperor did such damage to it. I did nothing. The Word did it all.

From such an activist as Luther, who lived the Reformation every bit as much as he taught it, this is no small understatement. It also discounts the conjunction of many other factors. As we have already considered, the church was long overdue to be challenged, however impregnable she looked. The time had come for everyday people to break out of feudalism. New horizons were constantly being discovered through great sea-faring exploits, opening many other new vistas of expectation. The age of print had just arrived. So too had 'back to the text' scholarship that enabled the message of scripture to be re-discovered. It was indeed a most favourable moment in history, without which the Reformation could not have happened. But, as Luther knew, what happened was far more than an accident of history. In the final analysis, it took the Word of God to bring His story into history. Without that, for all the conjunction of events coming together in that particular moment of medieval history, the Reformation would never have happened let alone had the impact it did, across the nations and the generations.

Notwithstanding all his own formidable efforts, Luther knew that the power which had released the Reformation was *sola* power. It was of three sorts—*sola gratia, sola fide* and *sola scriptura.* Grace, faith, and scripture as the sole means of salvation. Though the "sun of righteousness" (Malachi 4 v2) had never ceased to shine, the ability to reflect its power had long since been lost. The result of Luther's struggles was to rediscover how to do so, that it might once more arise "with healing in its wings." As he did so, healing came to individuals, both in their spiritual condition, and also in their physical circumstances. And beyond individuals, even to nations.

What Luther unearthed was not just one verse of Romans buried in a thousand years of ecclesiastical rubble, but the central theme of all scripture—the righteousness and justice of God. As he came to recognise, it was not two themes but one that was to be celebrated. In the words of Jeremiah:

> "but, let him who boasts boast about this: that he understands and knows me, that I am the Lord who exercises kindness, justice and righteousness on earth, for in these I delight," declares the Lord.
>
> (Jeremiah 9 v24)

Luther clearly understood that Jesus Christ was the comprehensive fulfilment of this prophecy. He had come in the kindness and mercy of God. Also in Him was the empowering for God's will to be done on earth as it is in heaven. That not only all people, but all the structures of society, should conform to the just and righteous precepts of the God who is holy. For if in the Old Covenant there had been no division between social justice and private morality, then there could be no division in the New. He had paid for our sins, and carried the judgement on Himself, that we might be justified, and declared righteous. But manifestly God's free gift was not restricted to the needs of individuals. It was for the redemption of the whole of the created order—for society in its every expression, and for everything else that was to be found in life.

It was the well-deserved privilege of Luther to see the revelation of this not only in principle but also in practice even beyond his wildest imaginings and dreams. What he had discerned was that God's kingdom was about justice that was restorative, rather than retributive, and which applied to everything from the individual to the institutional. It was all to reflect the righteous justice of God, and proclaim His glory. All of life was to be *coram Deo*—life lived before God, in reverent submission to His word. Which, as subsequent events even in his own lifetime were to prove on an international scale, was not just theological treatise. It had tangible power to break through the dominance and the corruption that existed in the sixteenth century church, and much more besides. For it eventually impacted almost everything from education, science and the arts through to commerce and government.

Simply by enabling people to recognise that there was direct access to God by grace and through faith alone, came the release of a whole new understanding of the dignity of each individual. Out of this were to come massive political reforms in many nations, for there was no more basis for arbitrary government. It released huge energy for social reform, and amongst much else led to the abolition of slavery, and a new understanding of civil liberty. It broke down the division between the sacred and the secular, ennobling all work if it was done to the glory of God. Thus it paved the way for what came to be known as the Protestant work ethic, which considered commerce and profit acceptable, providing it was within the context of stewardship and social responsibility. The consequence of all this was a shaping of the character of the western nations that affects them to this day.

Never before or since has the nailing of one notice on a church door had such repercussion. At the time, even Luther had no idea of the mighty effect that *sola* power could have. Yet such is the potential of God's word, even through one man. For to an equally reluctant Jeremiah, God had said

> Now, I have put my words in your mouth. See, today I appoint you over nations and kingdoms to uproot and to tear down, to destroy and overthrow, to build and to plant.
>
> (Jeremiah 1 v9-10)

Such are God's ways of working to touch entire nations. They depend not on the strategic planning of humans, but simply on a tenacious willingness to seek out, and to speak out God's word. The question therefore is not whether a new season of reformation is possible in the situation the western church has now reached, for the sixteenth century Reformation proves what can happen in a situation that was even more corrupt. The operative question is whether it is willing to first address the words God has put in its mouth to itself, and to tackle the reasons for its own acquiescence. Which is not to deny all the good that remains within it. But if its acquiescence is not uprooted, then it can have no integrity for uprooting or tearing things down in nations and kingdoms. Indeed it risks discovering for itself the extent to which becoming a reproach and a byword, an object of ridicule and cursing, is still valid for today.

For though the corruption of the hierarchy of the late-medieval church far exceeded anything within today's church, it is possible that the opposite may be true regarding the acquiescence of its membership. In the pre-Reformation church there were many of the common people who were hungering for the fresh fruit of the gospel. But in today's world, there seems to be enough crystallised fruit left over from the past Reformation to satisfy most of those who are genuinely hungry. And at the same time, enough scope for sustenance to also be drawn from the indulgences of today. Not the sort that Tetzel had on offer, which were designed to shorten the journey to heaven after we die, but the new improved version designed to shorten the journey to our substitute heaven even before we die. Yet comforting as such modern-day material indulgences may appear, just as with Tetzel's variety they can lead to equally heavy bondage, for indulgences have never come cheap. Which is why so many of the western church's remaining membership live such driven lives, simply to earn the money they cost, though with so little awareness of just how much is being traded for that which is of no eternal worth. Let alone the fact that the pursuit of indulgences is addictive in itself.

For as Tetzel also knew, comfort can become terribly compulsive. Rather like the mouse that cannot get off its wheel, the only answer for the addict is to do it some more. But the more it is done, the less perception there is of what is being done. In this lies the story of the subversion of the post-Reformation church from its calling, as it became less and less able to fulfill what it was appointed for: which was to be against the world, for the world. Indeed, looking back, it appears that almost as soon as it was released from its delusion about old-style indulgences, it started buying into the new style. Forbidden fruit has quite a history of being rather more attractive than the good fruit that may be freely enjoyed, and so it was with the good fruit of the Reformation.

Chapter Three

Different Types of Light

"KNOW THEN THYSELF, presume not God to scan—the proper study of mankind is man." A rather different jingle from that of Johann Tetzel, but an equally revealing one at that. This time, however, proclaiming the ethos not of what preceded the Reformation, but of what followed it—the Enlightenment. Sometimes known as the 'Age of Reason', it inaugurated a critique of Christianity that was to cause much uncertainty in the western church. Not that the Reformers had no place for reason. Indeed, it was this very type of thinking that the Renaissance had opened up which had helped them to question the assumptions of their received traditions. Most crucially it had enabled the 'back to the text' study of scripture that had birthed the Reformation message. What the Enlightenment changed, however, was the place of reason, elevating it to a pre-eminence above all else. Epitomised supremely by the enthronement of the Goddess of Reason in Notre Dame in 1793, reason now masqueraded as an angel of light.[1]

Despite having a great many faces, the defining characteristic of the Enlightenment was the belief that there was nothing in this world that human reason could not penetrate. The human mind was therefore the indubitable point of departure for all knowing. Thus it viewed processes, not in terms of purpose, but in terms of cause and effect. It assumed that all true knowledge was factual, value-free and neutral. Over and against facts were values, which did not have the same objective truth about them. The holding of them was therefore a matter of taste, and religion was soon relegated into this category. With the assumption that all problems were solvable, the Enlightenment put high premium on progress, expansion, advance and modernisation, and such thinking led to exactly this. Science and medicine made quantum jumps, the concept of technology emerged, and material benefits were achieved without which we could not imagine life today. So dramatic and compelling were its advances, that the Enlightenment seemed to be able to define its own terms, and name its own price.

Yet, as so often can be the case in life, all that glitters is not necessarily gold. There was a spiritual downside to the exercise of reason as the Enlightenment had adopted it. For its roots were actually in Greek paganism. With the Renaissance had come the revival of classical learning by scholars, known as humanists. These people were to be distinguished from the humanists of the nineteenth century, who ideologically propounded a religion of man. The humanists of the sixteenth century were simply teachers of literature who did not have any one philosophical or religious position. However, whereas the Reformation rediscovered long-lost truth through the work of the humanists, the

Enlightenment rediscovered a long-lost deception. This was a very different experience of 'back to the text.' For out of the study of the classical writings was released the notion of the universe as a closed, physical system, controlled entirely by natural laws. By defining the laws which govern both earth and sky, the aim of the early Greeks was to get free from the fear of death and the power of superstition. It led to what has been called anti-religious materialism captured in the saying "Happy the man who can know the cause of things, and has trampled underfoot all fears, inexorable fate, and the clamour of greedy hell".[2]

One description of the re-discovered Greek paganism that had lain dormant in classical literature during the Middle Ages was that it was like the germ of some ancient plague in a tomb. When the humanists opened up the tomb, they did not realise the consequences of what they were releasing. For the material success of the Enlightenment seemed to validate the whole package of thinking that it brought. Pragmatically, it really did seem to work to treat the world as a closed system. No longer was there a need for an external reference to God, because it appeared that a truth that brought results could be found from within. All that was needed was to proceed from one point of reason to another. What was rather less clear was that this was a very blinkered march back into paganism, as if the windows of the house in which life was lived had been bricked up. There was no longer the opportunity to look out on that which was transcendent, nor for external light to shine in. The only illumination had to come from the artificial light within.

From then on that which had the potential to be the most amazing servant was allowed to become the dominant, all-demanding master. As reason was allowed to define the boundaries of the closed system, not only was spirituality put firmly outside, but the philosophy of secularism was also invited in. This resulted in the process of secularisation, through which from the centre outwards, successive sectors of society were cut adrift from the decisive influence of religious ideas and institutions.[3] Thus the relevance of God's precepts were progressively left out of everything from science to civil affairs. As was His grace. Faith was now in the power of reason, and in its ability to crack the code of the universe by discovering the scientific laws that sustain it. This became the new legalism of the dawning age. Nothing was to be sacrosanct or sacred, except reason itself. For all problems were ultimately reckoned to be solvable, given the application of sufficient systematic thinking. As this was done, so it claimed, reality could then be mastered.

Somewhat prophetically, on the day Luther stood trial at Worms, he made clear his own view of the place of reason. "Unless I am convicted by scripture and plain reason, I cannot and I will not recant." He did not belittle human rationality. In fact he acknowledged the place of reason in the process of theology. What he rejected however was reason as an independent source of authority alongside scripture. Yet the day in 1620 when René Descartes coined his famous dictum *Cogito Ergo Sum* - "I think, therefore I am" - was described by Archbishop William Temple as "the most disastrous day in European history." Descartes' exercise in rationalism had brought him to one bottom line conclusion. That there was only one thing he could not doubt - which was the fact that he doubted. At that point, he redefined being in terms of thought, and thereby began a trend that has not yet been reversed.

Indeed, it has been suggested that, as a result of Descartes, a new fall took place in a deeper way. For it led to the logic that because I think, therefore God is. Everything to do with God becomes subject to our judgement. The individual becomes the ultimate reference point in thought. No longer is man to be understood in the context of community, let alone in relation to God. Presume not God to scan, the proper study of mankind is man. All this was very far from the *coram Deo* of the Reformers, or their other great cry *Soli Deo Gloria*—'to the glory of God alone.' Yet it is this thinking which has continued to permeate the centuries ever since the Reformation. The holy, and holistic, world view the Reformers had fought for had been totally inverted by that of the Enlightenment. It brought a radical challenge to Christianity that has been passed on to us today. For in the most subtle and insidious way, each of us born into the western world are still brought up to venerate the benefits of rationalism, not realising what we receive and what we reject as we do so.

All this stands between us and the good fruit of the sixteenth century Reformation message as it was received in its day. Powerful as were the teachings and the writings of the Reformers, they were not principally addressed against this agenda. They were tackling a different malaise in church and society. Thus, if all that is hung on to is the crystallised fruit of the sixteenth century Reformation, it is not surprising that so many of the faithful suffer from what is sometimes called 'cognitive dissonance.' For there is a very marked gap between the faith handed down from the Reformers, which manifestly had such impact in its day, and the surrounding world view of today. In this, there are all too few bridging points between the sacred and the secular. They are apparently two different realms that coexist in parallel, but with a great chasm between.

Such is the legacy of the Greek paganism that the Enlightenment let back out of the box. It generated a whole new agenda, that the re-discovered gospel as it was applied in the sixteenth century was never directed towards. Not only was it a different agenda, but it was also a completely different set of presuppositions that were involved.So it was that, in the desperate attempt to cope with this, the presentation of the reformed gospel was adapted to the demands of secularism, and the bits that did not seem to fit were soft-pedalled or even removed.

The crunch came when in the wider attempt to uncover the rational roots of religion, the Enlightenment tackled the intellectual credentials of Christianity. It set up a confrontation between faith and reason, in which it presupposed the omnicompetence of human reason. It proposed that the beliefs of Christianity should be seen as completely rational, and therefore capable of standing up to critical examination, though not in the classic tradition of God's revelation being the frame of reference within which all other reality is interpreted. Instead it inverted the tradition, so that human reason was to be the context in which claims to the knowledge of God had to be justified. Such use of reason led to treason.

For it then applied scepticism, if not outright distrustful suspicion, to any claims about divine intervention into our physical world. In so doing, it questioned the previously held understanding of God's relationship with the world. Human reason, according to the Enlightenment, should become the final arbiter of any claims of revealed knowledge of God. Its supposed objective was to liberate thought from the unexamined assumptions of the religious communities. But that also made it both judge and jury.

A further assault to be handled was the evolution of history as a critical science. This established the relativity of all human projects, including religion of any sort. With such a view of history, the Christian faith found it hard to maintain its claim to the overarching interpretation of all human history. If the Christian religion was set inside the historical process, rather than having the external standpoint afforded by revelation, then how could it offer direct access to any transcendent reality? Thus, the argument went, Christian knowledge of God had to be seen within the limitations of all human activity. It could no longer lay claim to absoluteness.

Here was fundamental conflict indeed. For there is no reasonable reply if our conviction is that the only way to understand the mystery of God is through revelation or that man's reason, being at the least corrupt, if not the victim of total depravity, is incapable by itself of coming up with correct answers. It was a whole new critique of orthodox Christian belief which challenged not just the nature of its theological heritage, but the very plausibility of it. Conducted, it should be noted, with a ferocity that had no precedent. It was a challenge that the Reformers of the sixteenth century would doubtless have sought to address. Yet this was not the agenda they were facing when they hammered out the reformed doctrine. It therefore offered little defence against the Enlightenment world view, such that the impact on doctrine was profound, and continues to be. Some of which was as follows:

1) Scripture. The Bible, it was said, was to be treated just like any other book. This was insidious enough, no longer differentiating it from other types of literature. But it was then subjected to extreme critical scrutiny, both literary and historically, far beyond that which would be applied to any other literature. Thus the status of the Bible was shifted from being the supreme and eternally reliable source of revelation, to become something lost into a much bigger scheme. From this emerged a criticism of the Bible that has not ceased to evolve.

2) Jesus Christ. The conclusion of Enlightenment thinking was that there was a great discrepancy between the real Jesus of history, and the New Testament interpretation of his significance. Whilst the idea of a supernatural redeemer was unacceptable to rationalism, the idea of an enlightened moral teacher was not. Thus began a quest for a simpler, more human Jesus, more acceptable to the spirit of the new era. One whose authority should henceforth lie in the quality of his teaching, rather than in being God incarnate, and whose death on the cross was to be re-interpreted as no more than an example of the highest self-giving. This, however, was far removed from the way in which God forgave the sins of mankind, particularly as the Enlightenment gave no credence to the resurrection as an historical event. The whole understanding of atonement therefore became subject to criticism.

3) Miracles. With the new emphasis on mechanistic progress, there was also increasing scepticism about the possibility of miracles. This was used to further erode the credibility of scripture, and especially the authenticity of the Jesus of the scriptures, who was so identified with them.

4) Original Sin. The idea that human nature was in some sense flawed was fiercely opposed by the Enlightenment. The thesis of Jean-Jacques Rousseau, for example, was that human beings were noble savages who were good, equal and free. So it was considered oppressive to talk in terms of original sin. Such talk was something mankind needed to be set free from. Thus a direct challenge was made to the doctrine of redemption which presupposed the very opposite, that mankind's greatest need is to be liberated from the power of original sin.

5) The Problem of Evil. Whilst in the medieval period, the existence of evil did not threaten the coherence of

Christianity, the Enlightenment turned it into a challenge to the credibility of Christianity. Hence in Voltaire's *Candide* the satirical refrain, "all for the best in the best of all possible worlds." It was this that provided the basis for a fashionable religion of the period—deism. In it, God was defined as the great clockmaker who had designed the universe and set it going, but is now leaving it to run down. Any further intervention was just to be regarded as superstition.

6) Revelation. This was now deemed to be superfluous since natural religion, understood in moral terms, should contain all that is of value in a supposed supernatural revelation. By contrast with the absolute value the Reformers placed on the truth that God had revealed in scripture, the Enlightenment now posed the most critical challenge to God's revelation of Himself in Jesus Christ.

However, it was not only the challenge of the thinkers that the church had to face. Despite all their arguments, it could be said that they were just weaving abstract concepts with words. So one response was to say that if faith and reason were in conflict, then so much the worse for reason. However, there then emerged another formidable opponent to contend with, in the form of science. Its new discoveries presented a strong case for saying the very opposite. If faith and reason were in conflict, so much the worse for faith! For science began to suggest that the Bible, at least as it was then interpreted, was wrong. Initially Copernicus and later Galileo, despite the condemnation of the Inquisition, came to the conclusion that the earth revolves around the sun. This was the opposite to what the Bible seemed to say. Then came the geologists, whose studies of rocks and fossils left them struggling to get creation into a seven day event in the year 4004 B.C. Added to this was Darwin's theory of evolution which brought further difficulties, and so on. Whatever the inability of science to speak into matters of morality, it served to strengthen the Enlightenment critique, not just of the Bible, but of all the revelation that was drawn from it.

Thus it was that the church found itself in a rear-guard situation, defending itself as best it could. But by its very nature, Protestantism was vulnerable to taking on board at least a measure of the thinking of the Enlightenment. Being itself birthed through an independence and creativity of thought, there was actually a certain appeal in such thinking. And because of this resonance, Protestant theology took up a degree of alignment with it and found little to officially resist the move. For unlike the authority of the centralised structure that the Roman Catholic church still had, the Protestant ecclesiastical institutions of the time were relatively powerless.

So despite many inconsistencies in the rationalism on which the Enlightenment was based, it was still highly corrosive to the faith that the Reformers had so tenaciously fought for. It caused much uncertainty at the time, and the backwash has affected western Christianity ever since. Because the adequacy, if not the veracity, of the gospel was called into question the church became timid in telling again 'the old, old story.' One commentary on the long-term effects of Enlightenment thinking on the church in the western world puts it like this:

> Secularism's greatest success, however, is in the widespread demoralisation in the ranks of the clergy and theologians who are supposed to proclaim and interpret the truth of the gospel but delude themselves that they are achieving that purpose by adapting Christian faith and life to the demands of secularism.[4]

All of which helps explain the condition in which the western church now finds itself. It also highlights how much must happen if it is ever to recover the gospel as that which can alone reform the life of the nations.

Battle for the Hilltop

Built on the top of a hill, the old city of Geneva is a microcosm not only of what followed from the Reformation, but also of what followed from the Enlightenment. For not only did John Calvin spend some rather notable time there, but so too did Jean-Jacques Rousseau. Arguably the most influential thinker of the eighteenth century, his radical and secular theory of government has profoundly influenced revolutionary thinking ever since. His thoughts contributed significantly to what led up to the French Revolution, and indeed to other revolutions. Voltaire was also intimately connected with the way Geneva thought in the eighteenth century, and his writings were a further contribution to the atmosphere which led to the revolution France was later to experience. Vladimir Lenin studied there as well, presumably with the seeds of soviet socialism already evolving in his mind.

That same hill top has therefore witnessed not just the thinking of reformation, but also of revolution. It is as if the hill top has been, and still is, a loud speaker to the nations. Which explains the spiritual battle that has since been fought over who gets to speak from the top of it. Indeed, it may well offer a vital insight into why, when some remarkable expansion is happening in the world-wide church, Britain and Europe, the home of the sixteenth century Reformation, should be so stuck. For it points to a much greater battle, in which there is not only reformation, but also retaliation.

Today, Geneva's landmark is the *Jet d'Eau*. Rising 130 metres, the spectacular fountain dominates the lakeside view of the city, symbolising its international prominence. Yet it is rather more about appearance than reality. Though the area it stands in is called *Eaux-Vives,* meaning Living Waters, the spiritual significance of the name has long since been lost. Indeed the words ring out from the prophet Jeremiah, of whom there is a statue just a few hundred metres away up on the hill of the old city:

> Be appalled, O heavens, at this, be shocked, be utterly desolate, says the Lord, for my people have committed two evils; they have forsaken me, the fountain of living waters, and hewed out cisterns for themselves, broken cisterns that can hold no water.
>
> (Jeremiah 2 v12,13 R.S.V.)

Later, he speaks again of what would happen to those who, having drunk from the fountain of living water, forsake the Lord. They would be "put to shame" (17 v13). A prophetic warning in every age to every believer and also to every church and every denomination.

What began to follow the Reformation a century later, on the very hill top on which the old city of Geneva is built, was exactly this. As in the time of the prophet, it was again about the temptation to dig out cisterns. Few in Jeremiah's time, or in 17th century Geneva, might have seen it in this light at the time. Yet, whatever else it appeared to be, this was what the prophet saw. Intellectual cisterns were being constructed that would apparently result in an extraordinary benefit. By human effort, the living water of wisdom could be stored on man's terms, and then used as he determined. It was about getting what was thought to be the water of life under human control, entirely contained in their own minds. Such cisterns, so they thought, would always be overflowing. No more would they need to depend on an external fountain either. A very attractive proposition indeed, so it appeared.

In the final analysis, the philosophical and intellectual cisterns that were constructed during the Enlightenment were simply unable to hold the true water of life. What was left from the Reformation seeped away through the breaks and cracks that permeate even the best of human reasoning. But there was now no source to replace what had been lost. So from the city on the hill where the high message of Reformation had sounded forth to neighbouring cities and nations, a counterfeit then followed. In spiritual terms, whatever material advances it brought, it led only to deformation. As the Lord said to Jeremiah:

> Have you seen what faithless Israel has done? She has gone up on every high hill and under every spreading tree and has committed adultery there.
>
> (Jeremiah 3 v6)

In place of the three great *solas*, grace, faith and scripture as the sole means of salvation, the Enlightenment propounded its one and only *sola*, which was by reason alone. The need for grace was obviated, as according to the Enlightenment, man did not suffer from original sin. It was not a gift of God that he needed, because human progress was achievable by his own efforts. Faith had been made to bow its knee to reason, as had the revelation of scripture, which itself had come under the severest criticism. Reason was now declared to be omnicompetent, and the yardstick by which all else was to be judged. Therefore God withdrew His light from the city, again to the echo of Jeremiah's words:

> My people are fools, they do not know me. They are senseless children; they have no understanding. They are skilled in doing evil; they know not how to do good. I looked at the earth, and it was formless and empty; and at the heavens, and their light was gone. I looked at the mountains, and they were quaking; all the hills were swaying. I looked, and there were no people; every bird in the sky had flown away. I looked, and the fruitful land was a desert; all its towns lay in ruins before the Lord, before his fierce anger.
>
> (Jeremiah 4 v22-26)

Apart from a short period of evangelical revival in the early nineteenth century, God has not in any great measure restored His spiritual light to the city of Geneva. *Sola* power needs the light of the Sun, and however much reason can masquerade as an angel of light, it cannot reproduce for itself that light which alone comes from on high. Such light as remains in Geneva is simply the after-glow from its past—though even that is evidently still quite sufficient to continue to distinguish it amongst the cities of the world.

Looking at the state of the western church today, the fact that it lacks power to impact the nations suggests that rationalism still has a far greater influence in it than we might realise. As in the city of Geneva, there remains a certain after-glow, but that is not true Light. Even woven into our Christian thinking is the thinking of the Enlightenment, illustrated by the familiar emphasis on 'personal salvation.' Though faith has to centre initially on an individual, if it goes no further, then it simply reflects the individualism of the Enlightenment that places individual man at the centre of everything. Christian experience can then be reduced to no more than the meeting of our personal needs, and when this happens, it misses the most basic point of Christian commitment, that we are saved in order to serve. Though the criteria of how much our felt needs are being met by God can yield a certain fair-weather commitment, it is not the basis for a valiant army. There is a battle to be fought for each and every spiritual hilltop on which God's people should be standing, and only as we set about that will more of the true light of the gospel be reflected to the nations.

Duel, but not Dualism.

At one level the post-Reformation story of both Geneva and the western church could be explained by the tendency, sooner or later, for faith to atrophy. There is always an ebb and a flow of human enthusiasm, with the potential for a 'second-generation syndrome' that loses the immediate message and intellectualises the experience. At another level, the Enlightenment might be considered as the Renaissance back with a vengeance, for spiritual dynamics often do bounce back or even kick back, despite having been subjugated once. Given the extent of the sixteenth century Reformation, perhaps this is a sufficient explanation of a movement as powerful as the Enlightenment emerging in the following century. It can be explained as part of the swing, albeit a very big one, of the spiritual pendulum. But, at a higher level still, it can be seen as the reflection of a far greater spiritual battle, which cannot be completely explained by flesh and blood, but only by the presence of dark powers over this world, and spiritual forces of evil in the heavenly realms (Ephesians 6 v12).

Scripture is remarkably thin on describing how such forces actually work in their attempts to win back the spiritual hill tops. However tantalising it is to know more, it becomes an exercise in theological hypothesis to try to work out their structures and mechanisms. Indeed, scripture seems to imply that we are not meant to know, perhaps for our own good. What is made clear however is that though there is a duel that every advance of the kingdom of God involves, it is not about dualism. It is not about the outworking on earth of a battle between two equal spiritual powers, however much Satan's power to counter-attack may suggest it is. The western church does not, therefore, need to remain as bound as it is, still having to argue its way out of the corner that the Enlightenment has boxed it into. Even if the lie was bought that reason was omnicompetent, the lie does not also have to be bought that Satan is. He is not equal with God in his power to intervene in the world, however much he would like to make it seem the case. With such perspective on the boundaries of Satan's power, the limits of the Enlightenment to bind the individual, the church and the nations are exposed.

One comment on the repeated reference to the title of Satan as the "prince of this world" (John 12 v31, 14v 30 and 16 v11) is particularly instructive.[5] The relationship Satan has with this world may have only been as a result of his rebellion. Alternatively, it could have been that in the beginning before the Fall, Satan might have originally been assigned by God some special task of the oversight of planet earth. Perhaps he was originally designated to have been God's angelic administrator of our earth. If so, did the rightful prince turn through rebellion into the usurper prince? Such an hypothesis would go a long way to explain the constant contesting of every spiritual hill top there is on this earth. Also to reassure us that this is as far as Satan can go, and only for a fixed time at that. Set that in the context of the one hundred billion or more galaxies that God has created, and we then realise that our perspective on Satan's ability to counter-attack might not be quite the same as God's!

In the first chapter of Job comes another vital insight. There we see a mystery of the heavenly realm revealed, at least in part. For though Satan is presented in scripture as no more than a fallen angel thrown out of heaven because of his pride (Isaiah 14 v12-14), yet he was still allowed by God to test Job and on Job's response, the outcome depended. Now apparently Job was blameless and upright, he feared God and shunned evil. However, the extent to which Satan was allowed by God to test him did not end with the total loss of his possessions, his sons and his daughters. Ultimately, Satan was permitted to put onto Job a disease which only stopped short of that which would take his life.

Though the mystery of suffering is huge, for our present purposes we simply note the fact that though Job was so righteous, this did not exempt him from such testing. Indeed, it was as if his righteousness actually qualified him to be a prime candidate. What is more, God was willing to risk sacrificing the most eloquent testimony of blessing He had on earth at the time, in order for a yet greater testimony to emerge. Which did indeed happen when Job's subsequent restoration came, though not through him first getting hold of an explanation for what had happened. Instead, it came through the very opposite experience, as he simply humbled himself before God saying "Surely I spoke of things I did not understand, things too wonderful for me" (Job 42 v3). Here was the triumph of faith over reason, which God then greatly honoured.

The story of Geneva, and indeed of the western church, is not out of keeping with this perspective, though it has yet to have the same ending. For God will allow the testing by Satan of that which has been the best, apparently right up to the point of destruction. Yet Satan apparently has only one real strategy for doing this, which, from the garden of Eden onwards, has always been the same: "Did God really say?" (Genesis 3 v1). The most basic temptation of all was to question the word of God with the reasoning of the mind. It all seemed so plausible to Adam and Eve, as it did in the process of rationalism in the seventeenth century. Yet the flaw then, and now, has always been the same: the moment the word of God is subordinated to human judgement, the recognition of God's truth as being the absolute determinant is destroyed. As the events which followed the Enlightenment illustrate so clearly.

"You will not surely die" are the words that consistently follow the experience of temptation. What the tempter sought to do in Adam and Eve was to displace the image of

God in them. Even if he could not destroy it completely, his goal was to deform them spiritually, as well as the place where they lived. So that neither they nor their surroundings would truly speak of the unspoilt glory of God. Meanwhile, Satan reassured them that it was not just legitimate, but indeed in their best interests, to say "We know best." That the judgement of their minds really should be the final arbiter of truth. But in doing so, he lured them away from an upright looking to the word of God as the absolute statement of truth. Then, without that heavenward perspective, he bent them in on themselves. To cause them to seek to define truth from within. To create an internal container, or cistern, for their new perception of truth and, in the process, to render them fickle and malleable for his fallen purposes. The consequence in Eden was the loss of grace. No longer was the fountain of living water theirs to drink from, without cost. This is the story that has been re-cycling itself ever since.

Throughout the ages, there have been greater and lesser reformations and retaliations, of which Geneva is a particular instance. But scripture tells of that time when Satan will have no more power to retaliate. Despite his on-going ability to exercise power in this world, he is already a defeated foe because in no sense does he have an equivalent status with the sovereign, omnipotent God. Satan can do nothing to prevent that end time when the thirsty will be given from the fountain of the water of life without payment (Revelation 21 v6 R.S.V.) But until then, the consequences accumulate in both church and society of many generations of Satan's questioning "Did God say...?" and only reformation has the power to deal with them.

Chapter Four

Modern Times

JUST AS JEREMIAH AND CALVIN addressed the spirit of their age, so in our modern times there are those who do the same. But rarely with any vision for Reformation. One example is the rock singer, Freddie Mercury, whose statue stands at the opposite end of the lake from Geneva, staring back aggressively at it. Revered as an icon of today's throw away society, he once said "My songs are like Bic razors. For fun. For modern consumption. You listen to it, like it, discard it, then on to the next. Disposable pop." He reflected the spirit of our modern, consumerist age, and both his life and his premature death in 1991 were like a counterpoint to the words of Jeremiah,

> Hear and pay attention, do not be arrogant, for the Lord has spoken. Give glory to the Lord your God before He brings the darkness, before your feet stumble on the darkening hills. You hope for light, but He will turn it to thick darkness, and change it to deep gloom.
>
> (Jeremiah 13 v15-16)

Mercury's mentality not only epitomised the thinking of our times, but also what follows from it. For in every age, belief begets behaviour, and ideas have consequences. The stumbling in the darkness that now characterises western society is no coincidence: it is simply the result of the presuppositions that its thinking is based on. The consequence is that beyond all the hype of a new millennium, there is rather less hope. Behind all that seems to gleam, is a backcloth of gloom. The challenge to the church is therefore to bring in the light which modernism promised so much of, but has failed to deliver. This may also be part of that conjunction of events which points to the possibility of a new season of Reformation. For it is when the darkness is at its greatest, that the light has the most potential to be seen.

Despite the pervading gloom, we first need to acknowledge that not everything which emerged out of the Enlightenment, and the modernism it led to, was gloomy in itself. "Daring to know" as Emmanuel Kant put it, resulted in many good things. Much benefit came from the marriage brought about between technology and market economics, which though a rational rather than a romantic match, nonetheless bore a child. Its offspring was the industrialism which was to bring the unimagined material benefits our lives now depend upon so heavily. But also to bring the equally unimagined negative effects that were so inextricably bound up with those benefits. Few though would ever want to return to a nineteenth century standard of living, let alone to that of the feudal society which existed before the Enlightenment. Some vital distinctions therefore need to be made, for it is not necessarily the things of the modern world that by themselves have caused the gloom.

Indeed much gleams in a way that only God could have enabled it to. For it was He who provided the raw materials for mankind to discover, and to be blessed by. Industry was even something Jesus Himself put His seal of approval upon. For what the incarnate Christ told us to consecrate and take in remembrance of Him were not corn and grapes, but bread and wine. Things in which the dirty hands of work have evidently played their part. The problem however is that in a fallen world, ecology and economy do not sit comfortably together, and goods have a remarkable tendency to become gods. Industrial advance unavoidably brings a complexity of its own, both materially and spiritually. Yet the vast quantities of mineral resources contained in the earth are surely there for a reason, given to be exploited by man. The implication is that man was meant to work through the complexities this would lead to, honouring his god as he did so. So whether it resulted in gloom or glory would simply reveal who the god was that he was truly serving—the natural god of a rational closed system, or the supernatural God of eternity.

It also means that there is nothing in our modern world that cannot be consecrated to Him. Providing we acknowledge who is the ultimate technologist and that the whole realm of science depends on principles God first wove into the fabric of our planet. As the Reformers put it, man should see himself as "thinking the thoughts of God after Him." But it is the absence of such an acknowledgement that has led to the gloom behind the gleam. The problem is not in the things of our modern times, but in its thinking. For it is an unlikely admission of the secular mind that God is the supreme technologist, under whose absolute orders we are to work. Modernity is therefore not so much the problem as the secular mind-set with which its problems have been approached. It was this mind-set into which industrialism, and its bed-fellow consumerism were birthed, carrying consequence to its third and fourth generation and, they in turn, to their own third and fourth generations. Landing many issues into our laps that we did not conceive, but which nonetheless are now our responsibility to resolve.

One influence that shaped the modern secular mind-set was existentialism. As a residue of the Enlightenment, it emphasised the immediate, lived experience of the individual. It was typified in Nietzsche's declaration "God is dead." He was saying that no one could, or indeed should, believe in God because He just wasn't relevant any more. It therefore gave permission to mankind to act without regard to the external claims of God. Which meant that he could claim technology as his very own brain-child, and operate it on the terms he thought best. So the Christian faith became increasingly relegated to the realm of personal, private opinion rather than being applied to the key issues of the day. The concept of *Soli Deo Gloria,* let alone the *sola* power the Reformers had re-discovered, was deemed to be nothing to do with the emerging cut and thrust of life. From here on, it was just for the stagnant backwaters of modern society. There it could still be considered privately engaging, even if it were socially irrelevant.

The consequence was that there was no external frame of reference to which the advances of industrialism were submitted. They were given free run, and they took over, driving mankind harder and harder as they did so, giving no time to think about his thinking. The economics of the market place became the final determinant, rationalised by the progress it seemed to be bringing. The age of steam became the incarnation of the age of reason, and the treadmill began to spin yet faster. It was not long, however, before a reverse take over occurred, when instead of technology being made for man, man became made for technology.

So it was that secularism secured a greater and greater place in our thinking. There was nothing to resist it, because there was no mechanism for integrating, let alone confronting, the secular with the sacred. Just as it was in the time of the Greeks, there was a profound divide between them and the lack of any effective bridgehead prevented the most essential dialogue of all from taking place. No effective explanation was forthcoming as to how to consecrate all these new things to the glory of God. So, into that vacuum, came the value systems of our modern times. Mankind hoped they would bring light, but instead they opened the door, as Jeremiah had prophesied in his own day, to thick darkness and to deep gloom.

From Optimism to Pessimism

Despite the material progress of the twentieth century, on balance it has only led to loss of hope. For it is with a far less optimistic attitude that we enter the new century, and indeed the new millennium, than we did the twentieth century. Mobile phones and the world-wide web would have been almost inexplicable to our Victorian ancestors. But what may have been even harder to explain would have been the increasing sense of hopelessness with which the twentieth century was to end.

Optimism was a fundamental tenet of Enlightenment thinking. It was based on the doctrine of perpetual progress that man's thinking would lead to. It pointed to Utopia at the end of the rainbow, if only it could be reached. For the Victorians, this was the order of the day. Then on into the twentieth century, the ever increasing speed of change continued to bedazzle. Modernity, as the industrial system based on a scientific world-view came to be known, consistently delivered the goods. Its outworking was everywhere to be seen. From travel, by land, sea and air, to home comforts and domestic appliances, or to radio and telephone, television and computers, it has thus far never failed to hold out the prospect of the next latest thing.

Certainly the endless flow of latest new things has given an illusion of perpetual motion. But it has not led to perpetual progress. A paradox to the secularist mind, but material indulgences have manifestly not been the answer to everything, despite the obsessive consumerism of the twentieth century. One of the biggest give aways is the indispensable role of advertising for markets to be created, and for the perception of need to be implanted into consumers. Otherwise how else can the whole thing be kept going? Only one small step back is needed to see what commentary this is on the superficiality of our modern times. Even without that step back, the inadequacy of the proposition that underlies it all is not hard to spot. That what will really satisfy the cry of the human heart is not God, but just that bit more—more size, more quantity, more quality, more whatever. Despite diminishing returns, the pursuit of happiness remains the aim. But whether pushing on in the same old direction will actually get us there is now rather less certain. For the moment, the band-wagon keeps on rolling. There is little alternative, because the secularist mind-set is so deeply etched into our thinking. Gone, though, is the unbridled optimism with which the twentieth century began.

One effect of modernity has been to mask the reality of mankind's hopelessness from him. It has kept him busy, and given him something to go for. Change has never been easy to cope with, yet almost by definition, it has been believed to be for the better. But the more modernity has failed to satisfy, the more its presuppositions are now open to question. Just how overoptimistic was it to suggest that all problems were solvable given enough thinking? What about the exclusion of religious experience, on the basis that it was contrary to the intrinsic nature of man? What about the fact that individualism evidently does little for community life? Or that the need to know ourselves can only be met by knowing ourselves in relation to others? The hollowness of the mechanistic view of life, as it views everything purely in terms of cause and effect, has been exposed. For the price of so-called progress has been the erasing of any greater sense of purpose. It has reduced life to the level of a person who can take a watch apart and re-assemble it, yet without any concept of time. There is no need to know what the machine is for. Simply to know what makes it tick is deemed to be an adequate view of truth.

When Bishop Lesslie Newbigin returned to Great Britain in the nineteen-seventies, after thirty years as a missionary in India, he felt the prevailing pessimism acutely. No longer was it a nation of faith, but a country in deep need of mission. The impact of secularism, played out in the theatre of modernity, had in his view brought the western industrialised nations to the point of decay. He wrote:

> It would seem to be proved beyond doubt that human beings cannot live in the rarefied atmosphere of pure rationality as the Post-Enlightenment world has understood rationality. There are needs of the human spirit which simply must be met. It seems that those religious bodies which have tried to accommodate as much as possible of the rationalism of the Enlightenment are those which are in decline, and that those which have maintained a strong emphasis on the supernatural dimension of religion have flourished.

He went on to cite the enormous growth of astrology amongst the most developed of societies, arguing it to be evidence that the human spirit cannot live permanently with the form of rationality which has no answer to the question 'Why?' [1]

What has most caused that question to be asked are the crises of the twentieth century. Before the century was a quarter of the way through, deep disillusionment was already setting in. World War 1 had seen the atrocities of trench warfare, and the death of nearly ten million soldiers. It had been the war to end all wars, but Utopia was no more just around the corner. Then followed World War 2. The Holocaust and the ending of it with the nuclear extinction of Hiroshima and Nagasaki deepened the disillusionment yet further. It was the application of the highest technology that had made this possible and also to enable more wars to be fought, and more people to be killed in this century than in any other. There have certainly been short-term bursts of optimism through the century, but planet Earth now feels a much less safe place. Not a few now wonder what we will all die of first. Will it be famine, ecological crisis, or the Bomb. And before then, how many will have died of AIDS?

But with the crumbling of the foundations of Enlightenment thinking it is not certain what, if anything, is replacing them. Some consider that we are in an overlap between two secular ages, in a transition between a dying and an emerging world-view, that is being described as post-modern. Its title is both apt and disturbing, for it suggests a despairing confession, that can only define itself by what it is not. A confession which offers no explanation of who or what we are, but only of where we have come from. A confession that is not about the dawning of a new era, but about the expression of a day without a tomorrow, and of a time without a future.

Post-modernism has been described as the reflection of conscious ignorance. It is the consequence of having tested the doctrines of the Enlightenment to destruction; finding them wanting, but having little else to replace them with. With the rejection of the classical thinking of antiquity, that truth comes by revelation, man had favoured modernism, with its promise that we can discover truth for ourselves. But now that modernism is on its way out, man doesn't have much left. So it's easier to speak of what we don't know, than what we do. Hence the language of the void, that sees only chaos out there. A chaos that an age of management and systems analysis can bring a measure of control to. A chaos that can even be rationalised by chaos theory, but a chaos that is still chaos.

Even without a Christian construct, some would argue that this may be unduly negative. For when, in the past, cultures have come to the end of their life-cycle it has happened over a much longer period of time. All that is happening now, it is reckoned, is the emergence of a new culture, accelerated by the thrust of electronic media. Our expectations of it may therefore be premature, and in time, all may get clearer. But even with this most favourable view, the fact remains that a massive cultural transition is going on in the western world, that is not easily interpreted, and the hopelessness of man is now not so easily masked.

The diversity of post-modernism adds to the difficulty of understanding what is going on. Some consider it to be easier to experience than define—an attribute also applied to Romanticism in an earlier age. But post-modernism is a very different kettle of fish. For it is that which is emerging from the lost glitter of the gods of science, technology and industrialism. It is something like the phoenix, the legendary Arabian bird which every five hundred years supposedly sets fire to itself and rises from its ashes. The sources of the ashes of western society are clear. They are the growing rejection of the capitalist dream and its values, despite the prosperity it has brought. Plus the disillusionment that it has not delivered world peace, social justice, personal satisfaction, or the secure future that it promised. Instead it has compromised not just the ozone layer but international stability as well. Meaning that, from here on, no one knows which country might threaten to destroy the world with a deadly weapon. It is the fire of that underlying loss of certainty that has turned so much optimism to ash.

Only time will tell quite what the phoenix will be like that does arise out of the ashes. But there are some clues. For whereas modernity was highly optimistic that humanity could solve its problems, post-modernity as it looks to the future, is pessimistic. So it just lives for the present and as it does so, it rejects truth as being revealed by God, or derived from scientific research. Like a spectre from the past, Descartes' principal of radical doubt also raises its head up out of the ashes. For once more, there is a fundamental disbelief in any claim to certainty. Individualism, however, continues unabashed. So truth becomes personal and known only through experience. Feelings and senses become its focal points, and even its determinants.

Post-modernism says "If it feels OK then it must be OK." So it can encompass different meanings for different people. Some see it as offering huge eclectic opportunities for gathering values and belief systems from here, there and anywhere, each having no greater claim to truth than the other: in the pluralistic world of post-modernism, what may constitute truth for one person might not constitute truth for another. Others see it as a formula for the fragmentation of society, that will be the consequence of the judgement that scripture warns about.

Jeremiah's Belt

Amidst all the 'not-knowing' that secular western society faces as it enters the third millennium, is the vexed question of what pluralism might do to it. In particular, whether it even has the power to hold society together. For though 'each to his own' can sound like a noble ideal, the reality would be very different. What every society needs in order to remain united is a common frame of reference. The fact that it may be as fallen a system as fascism or communism does not prevent it from fulfilling this role. But the absence of an all-encompassing frame of reference is a sure recipe for fragmentation.

The reason is that God created nations to be cohesive groups of people bound together by a common identity. God's highest purpose was that, whatever their cultural flavour, they would be held together by their shared relationship with Him. Israel was to be the supreme example of this. Which is why God called Jeremiah to act out a prophetic word that expressed the consequences of their discarding Him. The Lord told him to go and buy a linen belt, and put it round his waist, but not to let it touch water. This he did. Then the Lord told him to go and hide it in a crevice in a rock, which he also did. Later, the Lord told him to go and retrieve the belt from where it was hidden. But when he did so, he found it was ruined and completely useless. At which point the Lord said

> In the same way, I will ruin the pride of Judah and the great pride of Jerusalem. These wicked people, who refuse to listen to my words, who follow the stubbornness of their hearts and go after other gods to serve and worship them, will be like this belt—completely useless! For as a belt is bound round a man's waist, so I bound the whole house of Israel and the whole house of Judah to me, to be my people for my renown and praise and honour. But they have not listened.
>
> (Jeremiah 13 v9-11)

Jeremiah's belt can be seen as an Old Testament equivalent of the belt of truth in Ephesians 6 v14. It speaks of that gift of God which enables everyone, from individuals through to nations, to remain stable. To be held together, both humanly and spiritually, because 'united we stand, divided we fall' is ultimately a God-given principle of creation. Thus whilst pluralism may offer the illusion of true freedom, being open-minded about anything and everything, in reality, runs clean contrary to the way God has created the world to work. To quote G.K.Chesterton, the purpose of an open mind is the same as that of an open mouth. Which is eventually to close on something solid. It all suggests that if pluralism were truly to take over, then the outcome would be fairly predictable.

Some have suggested that western society is already a long way down this road. That we are increasingly finding ourselves living in what has been called 'a salad-bar society with no set menu.' The phrase 'pick and mix' is another that summarises the ethos of post-modern society.[2] Indeed with such a diversity of value systems already being embraced, an analogue of post-modern culture is that of shopping. The world and all of history is deemed to be like a vast supermarket, in which you can pick out the ingredients you like, and assemble them into your own version of something. And shopping is certainly one of the symbolic activities of our time. It may well matter less what you buy, than whether you had a nice time doing it. For this reason, shopping malls are now built like shrines of consumerism, if not cathedrals, that provide a sense of being to those that worship there. Enveloped by a multiplicity of goods and images, the shopper is supposed to experience a sense of true being—"I shop, therefore I am."

Another emerging motto of post-modern society is 'the medium is the message,' or even 'the medium is the massage.' Through television and the big screen, the members of the most advanced, industrialised society are increasingly being reduced to spectators. Arguably the most informed people there have ever been are passively, willingly and extensively being absorbed by a fantasy world of media-amusement. Apparently thinking ourselves free, we viewers are held captive to both the media and the message. It is they that become the new channel of the truth which purports to hold all things together. As the book age gives way to the screen age, society thus becomes ever more vulnerable to manipulation. Thereby, Satan is offered unparalleled opportunity to perpetrate a plethora of misleading, but very compelling lies. For the purposes of his destructive strategies, it is not even necessary that any particular one is believed. It is enough simply that we buy the concept of shopping around between them, and that it is pleasurable to do so. That if it feels OK, then it must be OK. Such is the potential of pluralism to deny the notion of absolute truth. Whatever other spiritual attire you wear, it declares that this particular belt is no longer in fashion. It is out of date. Other, that is, than in what can only be dismissed as the private backwaters of society.

Yet this gloomy scenario from the secular viewpoint may also provide one of those rare opportunities of history that only exists in the re-birthing phase of a culture. Not just for the regeneration of present-day values, but for values to be established that will shape the generations to come. For if pluralism does increasingly lead to fragmentation, then the search will be on in earnest for that which looks like a cohesive truth that can once more unify our western society. The question, however, is who will get to take the opportunity. The challenge for the western church is therefore how, in the mess of our age, to make the one true message stand out high above all others. Such that it will not be dismissed as just one more value system from which to pick and choose.

If this is to happen, it will need a church which is neither acquiescent, nor inconsistent, for both destroy the plausibility of the Christian message, despite its absolute truth. There should be neither a gap between its principles and practices, nor a dependency on the latest, new thing type of Christianity. All that this would achieve would be a competition with the out-going spirit of our modern age. It is not more innovation that is needed, but more renovation of that which comes alone through the repeated exercise of 'back to the text.' For there is no other way that the tendency, for example, to drift into a privatised understanding of Christianity that keeps it in the category of a spare time hobby, can ever be exposed. Such is the challenge to the reformers of the twenty-first century to make the gospel relevant to the agenda of the new millennium. Herein lies both the challenge and the opportunity, if not the defining point for where the next great battleground will be. For just as Satan was wheeling rationalism and secularism into place even as the sixteenth century Reformation was taking place, so too he would already appear to be taking up his position to contest the next great opportunity for reformation. This time through what is being called the New Age.

New Age—New Rage

By remarkable coincidence, the basis of the New Age is supposedly an astrological change, that just happens to overlap with the present cultural change. Its hypothesis is that each star lasts two thousand years. So in its theory, just as the Christian age of Pisces replaced the Judaic age of Aries in the first century AD, so two millennia later, the Aquarian age of psychic spirituality is now replacing Christianity. The attention it has drawn suggests that broad-based interest in spirituality is not declining in the way that main-stream church attendance suggests it is. That far from being on the wane, it is not just surviving, but is actually thriving. What it reveals is that the lie has not been entirely bought that God is just a make-believe answer in a meaningless world. Instead, it proves that mankind is incurably religious. Indeed, what is happening is the outworking of the saying that "secular man killed a God in whom he could not believe, but whose absence he could not bear." Despite all that has happened in the last five centuries, and especially in this last one, the hunger for a spiritual answer still remains.

Satan would appear to be well aware of this, and is therefore seeking to offer his new religious alternative, which is a very insidious one at that. For the New Age movement seeks to counterfeit what is promised in "the coming ages" (Ephesians 2 v6-7) when we will see in full what our minds can only begin to grasp now. The degree of response to it has been such that New Age is now assessed as the world's fastest growing spirituality. Not only this, but it is also reckoned to be already a multi-billion dollar business worldwide. An early statement of it came in the 1960's musical Hair. "This is the dawning of the New Age ... This is the Age of Aquarius..." Its origins go back to the discovery in the West during the sixties that the use of LSD and other drugs appeared to induce an expanded consciousness. Such 'trips' could result in an illusion of heightened reality—but then so too, it was also discovered, could certain techniques of eastern spirituality, or western occultism.

During the seventies came a proliferation of cults bringing consciousness-raising techniques that produced parallel results: disorientation from previous perceptions and beliefs, detachment, and a conviction that one was enlightened, and living on a new plane of reality. What began in a counter-culture coalesced with mainstream culture as New Age spirituality. It has been described as *pot-pourri* spirituality. Amongst its predominant features are eastern meditation, occultism, astrology, belief in re-incarnation, ancient gnosticism and the 'oneness' of everything. It mixes 'monism,' which teaches that man, God and everything else are one, with pantheism, which teaches that God is an impersonal force that permeates everything. Effectively it is teaching that 'all is one' and 'all is God.'

Its background inspiration are various forms of Hinduism and Buddhism. The eastern-orientated approach thus marks a radical shift for the western mind. Yet perhaps that is not surprising, but even predictable. For how else could Satan replace the god of Aristotle that he had used to replace the God of scripture? If rationalism is no longer going to be the answer, then mysticism, as its exact opposite, is the next obvious port of call. It is indeed a convenient fit for modern man, in its offer of self-actualisation. It appeals spiritually, if not materially, to the aspirations of the individualist for continuing progress. It also suggests it has answers for the pressing global problems of our times. For it is a common New Age belief that as more people are taught how to attain heightened consciousness and transformed values, humanity will release its own psychic powers and become in tune with the spirits and energies of the earth, and even of the whole cosmos.

The threat of the New Age needs to be exposed for what it is. It promotes the antithesis of Biblical values. Instead of absolute values and commandments, it promotes a relative and subjective morality. It promotes practices clearly forbidden in scripture. It is fundamentally in opposition to the God of scripture and to Jesus Christ. But what has been suggested as being the most insidious aspect of it is its potential to bring about a new form of totalitarianism. Not by the transformation of the world, nor by a revolutionising transmutation of society, but by attempting the transformation of human nature itself. [3] If this appraisal is correct, then what might follow could make the despairing confession of post-modernism look like quite an attractive place for society to have stayed.

It may be argued either that all this is nothing more than scare-mongering, or by total contrast that this is the ultimate strategy of the Anti-Christ. But either way, the real question for the western church is the same. If the New Age movement is only the counterfeit, just what is the real thing God wants the church to reveal to the nations at this time? For if Satan has had to wheel out such threatening artillery, does it not suggest that even the principalities and powers witness to the present window of opportunity, for good as much as for evil? For reformation as much as for decimation?

From a human viewpoint, even the futurologists are hesitant to predict what the emerging scenario will be as we enter the third millennium. Certainly the instability of modern times could result in atomic mishap, the return of fascism or Marxism, the collapse of the western economy, or even a descent into a new Dark Ages. But whilst the possibility of a new barbarism or apocalypse is very real, there could be another scenario altogether. Like the proverbial drunken English road, it is also possible that western society is merely meandering in a daze to nowhere in particular. To paraphrase C.S.Lewis, we do not know if we are in the early chapters of our story, or the last one. As indwellers of the story, we are only asked to expect and eagerly await its conclusion, and not to predict when it will occur.[4]

Yet wherever our todays are placed in the greater story, there is much which still points to an up-coming window of opportunity for a new season of reformation. For however gloomy things may seem to be from a secular perspective, God's heart is always to restore. Even amongst all his prophecies about the judgement of God, Jeremiah also spoke of the heart of God for restoration.

This is what the Lord says: "You say about this place, 'It is a desolate waste, without men or animals.' Yet in the towns of Judah and the streets of Jerusalem that are deserted, inhabited by neither men nor animals, there will be heard once more the sounds of joy and gladness, the voices of bride and bridegroom, and the voices of those who bring thank-offerings to the house of the Lord, saying,

'Give thanks to the Lord Almighty, for the Lord is good, his love endures forever.'

For I will restore the fortunes of the land as they were before," says the Lord.

(Jeremiah 33 v10-11)

Much will therefore hinge on how perceptive the western church can become about the times we are in, and the place it has itself come to. Otherwise it will simply be sucked into the journey which western society is travelling, into the gloom which may get much thicker yet. Exactly where in it some form of decimation might lie, no one knows. But there is no need for the western church to be held captive to that journey. For there is no inadequacy in its gospel which has proven its power not only to survive the centuries, but also to tame empires and nations. Indeed it is the glory of this unchanging gospel that a new season of reformation would again reveal.

Chapter Five

The Survival
of Revival

WHILE THE SO-CALLED ENLIGHTENMENT shrouded the influence of the Reformation, it was quite unable to prevent some other rays of light from breaking in. For alongside the story of what led into modernism and all that followed from it, was a parallel story, about what came to be called revivals. They are also part of the post-Reformation era that cannot be ignored, as they make for not only some thrilling reading, but also even seem to speak of days of heaven on earth. So much so that they blunted the thrust of rationalism because it simply couldn't explain the experiences people manifestly had had. Yet within that story are some tough questions. For the term 'revival' was not coined until the beginning of the eighteenth century, and moreover, as a noun, it is nowhere to be found in the Bible. Which is not to deny scripture's revelation of God's heart for bringing back life to that which was close to death or even dead. Plenty of synonyms for revival are to be found in scripture, as are stories about it, such as the account of the valley of dry bones in Ezekiel chapter 37. Nor is it to deny the amazing things God has done in subsequent church history to bring life back to individuals, nations and the church itself. But in His sovereignty, God has chosen not to give any explicit definition of what an event called revival actually should be. Instead, what we do have is the challenge to consider why what we have come to call revival is not happening in Britain or Europe at this present time.

There are other challenges that the experience of revivals also pose. Why is it that revivals can, for example, often begin with such suddenness, and end with an equivalent abruptness? And what should be made of the extraordinary phenomena which can be experienced in these sudden seasons when the Holy Spirit's presence is so powerfully present? These are real challenges indeed, and presumably permitted for a purpose. For they prompt us to look beyond the immediate, restorative effect revival can have on both church and society to explore the greater purpose God may have through them. Which I would suggest is to expose the true heart of the church and, in particular, its availability for God to do a yet more significant work through it.

Given the tendency of our age to analyse everything, revivals are often viewed in terms of cause and effect. This, though, can only ever be subjective, and can therefore be quite misleading. Experiences that happened in another time or place cannot be definitive. Let alone be considered sufficient to fill the gap in scripture about what revival really is about. All too easily they can be idealised, whilst the limitations, and the subsequent downturn that can follow, are often ignored. The implication can also be drawn that they represent the high-water mark of the church. So rather than being understood as a means to an end, revival becomes an end in itself. Despite all that is true about story of revival, the far broader perspective should also not be lost sight of. For God was working His purposes out to use the church to impact nations long before what we presently call revival began less than 300 years ago.

Revival has been defined in many different ways. J. Edwin Orr, probably the greatest authority on revival this century, says "the best definition of revival is 'times of refreshing from the Lord'." Jonathan Edwards, through whom the first Great Awakening in America originated in the 1740's, spoke of it as "the surprising work of God." In contrast to his view that revival is entirely a sovereign work of God was that of Charles Finney, who led the second Great Awakening. His view was that revival is not a miracle, but depends on the right use of constituted means. So for him, revival was the "renewal of the first love of Christians in which believers are awakened and sinners converted." These, and many other definitions, seek to summarise the occasions when very considerable numbers of unbelievers have been brought to profound conviction of sin, followed by dramatic experience of conversion and transformation of lifestyle. Times which have often, though not always, involved unusual physical manifestations such as weeping, shaking, loud cries and falling. With this almost invariably comes a new intensity of prayer and praise. So much so that the community locally and far beyond is left in no doubt about what is going on.

Revivals are therefore quite distinct from the progressive renewal of the church. This is experienced as a process, and is largely contained within the four walls of churches and conventions. Though some may think it feels like revival, it is not the same. Revivals are experienced as sovereign and sudden events that spill out into the world. They often have clearly defined starting and ending points. They are usually associated with a specific place, and yet frequently have an impact far beyond their location or their date. They are also usually associated with specific leaders, who have often had intense personal encounters with God, both in their conversions and in their anointing for public ministry.

So, for example, the first Great Awakening, centred on the ministry of Jonathan Edwards in Northampton, Massachusetts and started in December, 1734. He described the orthodoxy of the church to which he was called as "notional". Parishioners knew their catechism but few cared deeply about Christ. Instead they were absorbed by business and everyday life, and gave little attention to God. What deeply concerned Edwards was the ability they had to talk about Christian truth, even though they were manifestly out of touch with supernatural reality. He saw them as able to move pieces of theology around like markers on the map of a territory they had never visited.

When the revival began there, it was reckoned that more was achieved in one week than in the whole of the previous seven years. As it ignited neighbouring congregations, and they in turn ignited others, revival quickly spread through New England. It reached its peak in 1740, and by the time it ended in 1744 around 30,000 conversions out of the total population of 300,000 resulted, with 150 new congregations being formed. Despite the lack-lustre style in which Edwards delivered his hand-written sermons, and his tendency to stare at the bell-rope, the Holy Spirit moved mightily through his preaching. Indeed his famous sermon "Sinners in the hands of an angry God" is still referred to. Intense conviction of sin was very common among those who responded, and some were even convicted that they were not more convicted.

Progressively, the towns around Northampton were touched. The story of the town of Enfield which had seemingly been left untouched is described by a local historian.

When they went into the meeting house, the appearance of the assembly was thoughtless and vain. The people hardly conducted themselves with common decency ... Edwards preached on the words from Deuteronomy 32v35 "Their foot shall slide in due time." ... Before the sermon was ended, the assembly appeared deeply impressed and bowed down with an awful conviction of sin and danger. There was such a breathing of distress and weeping, that the preacher was obliged to speak to the people and desire silence, that he might be heard. This was the beginning of the same great prevailing concern in that place, with which the colony in general was visited.[1]

Another is the Second Great Awakening, which began in September 1857, when Jeremiah Lanphier began a prayer meeting in Fulton Street, New York in September, 1857. Despite the most inauspicious of beginnings, in the following year it was to touch almost every state in the nation of America, adding around half a million converts to the churches. In New York alone, 50,000 out of a population of 800,000 were converted. From there the blessing spread, prompting the revivals in 1859 in both Ulster and Great Britain, where a similar number were converted, and subsequently in Norway and Sweden, were another quarter of a million were converted.

The Welsh Revival of 1904-5 is a further example of what has been called 'accelerated grace.' Centred on Evan Roberts' ministry, it lasted from September 1904 to June 1905, spreading through many towns in Wales. Roberts described the anointing he personally received like this:

One Friday night last spring, when praying by my bedside before retiring, I was taken up to a great expanse—without time and space. It was communion with God. Before this I had a far-off God. I was frightened that night, but never since. So great was my shivering that I rocked the bed, and my brother, being awakened, took hold of me thinking I was ill. After that experience I was wakened every night a little after one o'clock. This was most strange, for through the years I slept like a rock, and no disturbance in my room would awaken me. From that hour I was taken up into divine fellowship for about four hours. What it was I cannot tell you, except that it was divine. About five o'clock I was again allowed to sleep until about nine. At this time I was again taken up into the same experience as in the earlier hours of the morning until about twelve or one o'clock ... This went on for about three months.[2]

The revival which arose out of the ministry of Evan Roberts eventually led to around 200,000 conversions. Jessie Penn-Lewis reflected the impact of what happened there like this.

The spirit of gladness and praise filled all hearts, as thousands rejoiced in a new found assurance of salvation. The Spirit of God did His own work of convicting, and many were the evidences of His power working through hymn and testimony. A young man would return his prize medal and diploma because he had gained it unfairly. A grocer would return money picked up in his shop, and kept although knowing the one who dropped it. Long-standing debts were paid. Stolen goods returned. Prize-fighters, gamblers, publicans, rabbit-coursers, and others of the class rarely touched by ordinary means came to Christ, and quickly the world knew the results. Magistrates were presented with white gloves in several places because there were 'no cases.' Public houses were forsaken. Rowdiness was changed to soberness. Oaths ceased to be heard, so that, it was said, in the collieries the horses could not understand the language of their drivers. The reading of light literature was exchanged for Bible reading, and shops were cleared of their stocks of Bibles and Testaments.

Prayer meetings were held in collieries underground, in trains and trams and all kinds of places. All the world bore testimony to these practical evidences of the power of God."[3]

The last revival to take place in Great Britain was in the Hebridean Islands, between 1949 and 1953. It began when the Presbytery on the Island of Lewis issued a statement concerning the unholiness of their churches at that time. What was needed, they said, was clear—repentance. Out of this came a group of people who responded and prayed for God to come upon them and their community in power. Through the ministry of Duncan Campbell, revival broke out on the islands of Harris and Lewis. One description of the impact it had was this:

When men in the streets are afraid to open their mouths and utter godless words lest the judgements of God should fall; when sinners, overawed by the presence of God tremble in the streets and cry for mercy; when, without special meetings and sensational advertising, the Holy Ghost sweeps across cities and towns in supernatural power and holds men in the grip of terrifying conviction; when "every shop becomes a pulpit; every heart an altar; every home a sanctuary" and the people walk softly before God - this is revival![4]

These few brief snapshots are just part of a picture that has emerged from around the world since the beginning of the eighteenth century. Often there has been a striking similarity in their character and the consequences, notwithstanding the differences of history, geography or culture. There is a deep sense of the presence of God, and an overwhelming conviction of sin against the God who is utterly holy. There is a profound certainty that only repentance about sin and trust in Christ's work on the Cross can bring reconciliation with God. Which is followed by a subsequent assurance of sins forgiven, with an empowering of the Holy Spirit to live out a God-honouring life thereafter. Notwithstanding the lack of a Biblical definition of revival, the impact of what happened in many different times and places is sufficiently parallel to invite a common explanation about it. But not only about its origin. For if it is a sovereign action of God who enables it, then another question also needs to be faced. Why is it that when so many extraordinary things happen in a season of revival that He only permits it to have a very limited survival?

Why do revivals cease?

Revivals can simply be described through the stories of the amazing things they typically lead to or they can be thought of in terms of the events they tend to involve. For they usually begin with some form of dramatic intervention by God, often on a specific date. So, for example, the Airport Vineyard at Toronto speaks about what began there on January 20th, 1994, and Brownsville Church, Pensacola about what began there on Father's Day, 1995. Next comes a unifying of otherwise diverse individuals and churches, which is followed by the third phase of the process. This is the recognition of the truths God has highlighted in His intervention, and the subsequent proclamation of them. Lives get revolutionised, and it is this which impacts families, communities and even nations. Finally, what has begun so suddenly frequently seems to come to almost as sudden an end.

Yet the consequences of a revival can reach far beyond its direct time frame or location. One of the most graphic of illustrations of this is the impact on 18th century Britain of what is sometimes called 'Wesley's Revival.' The social revolution that followed stands in the starkest of contrast to what happened in France during the same period. But even the lesser known revivals have often indirectly led to missions and outreaches that would have never taken place otherwise and the encouragement that their story gives to subsequent generations who may have lost vision is a legacy in itself.

It is against this greater perspective that the brevity of most revivals has to be set. If such tremendously beneficial consequences can result from revivals, why doesn't God sustain them so much longer, in order to anchor their consequences more strongly? Yet what Jonathan Edwards describes in *The Surprising Work of God* as "the gradual withdrawing of the Holy Spirit"[5] is something that every revival encounters sooner or later. Just as surprisingly as God intervenes, equally surprisingly, He also withdraws. Indeed one of the characteristics of the Great Awakening is that God's awesome presence would manifest itself in a place and then cease. Sometimes to recur again after a few months or years, and then finally to cease.

Beyond the question of why God works in this way is yet another question. Why is it that places where such amazing stories of revival took place should subsequently become so barren? Take for instance the subsequent spiritual decline in all but a few parts of Wales. Nowadays, it is hard to believe that this was where the greatest revival in Great Britain this century took place. Yet such is often the way with revivals. For a short time they are all about "Glory to the Father, and to the Son, and to the Holy Spirit" but it is not long before everything is "as it was in the beginning, is now and ever shall be; world without end, Amen." More perplexing still is the kick back effect that can go with revivals. Sad enough, and bad enough, are the unfortunate endings that some revivals experience, such as with what happened to Jonathan Edwards. For the church that had been so blessed by his ministry ultimately compelled him to resign when he started to impose restrictions on admission to communion. But worse still is the reversal of the process of revival that can follow in the decades to come, of which the story of Geneva is a graphic example. How, then, are we to understand not only the ceasing of revivals, but even their apparent reversal?

Firstly, there are the human explanations. Even in the Old Testament, there is a cyclical story over many centuries of restoration and decline, that can be explained, at least in part, in human terms. God-honouring Judges, and later Kings, were frequently followed by those who did not honour Him in the same way. It was a reality that Jeremiah knew so well. What repeatedly seemed to happen is that spiritual lethargy, and compromise with sin, set in to the times of renewal. This resulted in a turning away from God in the next generation, only to result in the loss of God's blessing. As affliction followed, there was a turning back to God in repentance and prayer, which was followed by the raising up of new leadership, through which restoration took place. It was a pattern that was repeated again and again.

This vulnerability of human nature to slide back into sin was something John Wesley also recognised. He once said:

> I fear, wherever riches have increased, the essence of religion has decreased in the same proportion. Therefore I do not see how it is possible, in the nature of things, for any renewal of true religion to continue long. For religion must necessarily produce both industry and frugality, and these cannot but produce riches. But as riches increase, so will pride, anger and the love of the world in all its branches.

Whilst such a diagnosis might explain the longer-term story of the city of Geneva, it does not, however, explain the abruptness with which the main phase of many revivals come to an end.

Other human factors may, however, contribute to it. The vulnerability of mankind to short-term enthusiasm is one, which leads to nothing more than spiritual immaturity. Jonathan Edwards used the analogy that "in the spring innumerable flowers and young fruits appear flourishing and bid fair, that afterwards drop off and come to nothing. So the same shower causes mushrooms suddenly to spring up as well as good plants to grow." Indeed in the parable of the sower (Matthew 13 v1-9) Jesus referred to the seed which fell on rocky ground, that sprang up quickly because the soil was shallow, but as soon as the sun came up, withered because it had no root. Enthusiasm, even as it spills over into fanaticism, may appear enormously encouraging at the time. The unfortunate fact is that it may be nothing more than self-centred emotionalism. The likelihood is that out of it will come the experience of large numbers falling away, bringing with it considerable potential to discourage others.

With this is the limited ability of the majority to stay in a spiritual high for any great length of time. One explanation of this is that for a short while, sin's potential to express itself is cut off. Like a volcano that has been capped, it might appear to have been brought under control. But it is only a question of time before it finds the next weakest point through which to release its lava. Unless the inner fire has been quenched, or in other words, the heart has been truly penetrated and the root of the personality touched, this will be inevitable.

Added to this is the limited ability of the leaders of revival to stay the course, with increasing demands and expectations coming upon them. The story of Evan Roberts' leadership of the Welsh Revival is one example. In retrospect, some have suggested that he relied far too heavily on a ministry of spiritual gifts rather than upon a ministry of the Word and that it was this lack of proper undergirding that resulted in a ministry more of exhortation than exposition, which he was unable to maintain. Moreover, the basing of revival on experience rather than exposition meant that his hearers were provided with only a limited basis for sustaining their own journey.

The danger of a personality cult growing up around a revival leader is another. It can arise as leaders begin to confuse their own inklings with God's leading. This can lead to pride, which can make them censorious, and eventually to a fall. Particularly if people are led into mistaking God's work for the leader's, which is something He will not tolerate. These, as well as other human factors, help to explain the considerable scope of the flesh and the world to cause revivals to cease, even quite suddenly. To them, however, must be added the third part of the triad, which is the role of the devil. For it is his personality that much account needs to be taken of in the sudden ending of revivals. Because the fact is that as revival progresses, the devil loses ground. It is not long before he also is awakened by what is happening. Some would even suggest that he is the first to wake up. And His response is to fight back in the classic ways that scripture speaks of—through infiltration, accusation and confusion.

In *Thoughts on the Revival in New England* (1742), Jonathan Edwards had already recognised the devil's strategy of sowing weeds among the wheat to discredit the whole crop, exactly as Jesus spoke of in Matthew 13 v24-30. He commented

> We may observe that it has been a common device of
> the devil to overset a revival of religion; when he finds
> he can keep men quiet and secure no longer, then he
> drives them to excess and extravagances ... Though the

devil will do his diligence to stir up the open enemies of religion, yet he knows ... that, in a time of revival of religion, his main strength shall be tried with the friends of it; and he will chiefly exert himself in his attempts to mislead them. One truly zealous person ... may do more ... to hinder the work, than a hundred great, and strong, and open opposers.

Alongside this strategy for de-railing a revival, Edwards also recognised another of the devil's strategies. This was the injection of spurious and disfiguring elements into it. He wrote: "Tis by the mixture of counterfeit religion and true, not discerned and distinguished, that the devil has had his greatest advantage against the cause and kingdom of Christ." By the subtle introduction of lies into a revival, or by re-inforcing its defects, the devil's aim is to confuse both the church and the world. To such confusion is then added the experience of everything from fierce criticism through to persecution, which Reformers like Luther and Calvin, and so many other leaders of genuine revival along with Edwards himself, have known to their great cost.

Beyond the overt local opposition to any revival is a hidden opposition of a greater order, which arose out of the driving underground of the Renaissance by the Reformation. When the Renaissance subsequently surfaced again in the eighteenth century, it successfully challenged the Reformation in a number of ways. One of the things eighteenth century rationalism persuaded western culture about was that the troublesome realm of the demonic could be dismissed as nothing more than irrational superstition. It enabled a demonic smoke-screen to be established, behind which the devil could operate his strategy of distraction and destruction. Ever since, the impact of rational thinking has blinded even the elect to the power of the devil to oppose any spiritual advance, let alone a revival, both overtly and covertly. But to quote Richard Lovelace, "there is no more contradiction between the combination of the world, the flesh and the devil in the production of decline than there is in the conjunction of environmental stress, physical strain and bacteria as causes of illness."[6] The explanation of the subsequent stories of Geneva, Wales and elsewhere, are deeply rooted in this triadic conjunction.

There may, however, be one more aspect to the sudden ending of revivals, that goes beyond the combined effects of the flesh, the world and the devil: the sovereign choice of God Himself. In fact, in that same extraordinary way Peter speaks in Acts 2 v23 of how God's sovereignty was outworked in the crucifixion of Christ through the deeds of evil men, so it may be with revival. Though from our perspective it is difficult to theologise how it works, it would seem that God can harness even evil for His purposes should He choose to.

Various analogies have been suggested to help explain why God might instigate revivals so suddenly, and equally surprisingly, allow them to end. One is that of a tornado, because it pictures the way the wind of the Spirit can come upon a community. Normally, the wind blows quietly and a steady stream of people are gently moved into the kingdom. A revival is more like a tornado from heaven which sweeps thousands into the kingdom in a very short space of time. Revivals can no more be created by human beings than a tornado. No one knows where tornadoes will start, or move to, or end. Yet everyone sees their effects, especially the cries for mercy of the penitent. [7] Certainly, this is an evocative analogy. As Spurgeon said, "We may put up our sails, but only God can make the wind blow." Yet it still does not help us understand why God should cause revival to start and finish so abruptly. Edward's thesis was that God sends revival when the church is at its worst and weakest. He wrote,

The church's extremity has often been God's opportunity for magnifying His power, mercy and faithfulness towards her. The interest of vital piety has long been in general decaying, and error and wickedness prevailing; it looks as though the disease were now come to a crisis ... When His church is in a low estate, and oppressed by her enemies, and cries to Him, He will swiftly fly to her relief, as birds fly at the cry of their young.

Perhaps the analogy of the electric starter-motor on a car engine may speak further into this aspect of revival. For although the internal combustion engine had not even been dreamt of in his day, Edwards may have appreciated the notion of God sending power to turn over the engine of the church for a limited season only. Not as a permanent mode of operation, but to see if the engine would fire as it was designed to, and maintain thereafter its own cycle of compression and combustion. If the engine doesn't then fire of its own accord, the operator may try again a few more times. If nothing then happens, he knows for sure that something needs attention.

So it may well be with God's attempts to start up the church with bursts of revival power that have gone on ever since the Reformation. It implies that God not only wants the engine of the church to be running, but for the church also to be in gear and moving forward once again on the journey of reformation it has started on but has yet to complete. Like with the sound of a starter motor in a car which won't start, perhaps God wants His church to realise that something needs to be repaired, so that next time the engine is cranked up, it will keep running as it was intended to. Then there will be sufficient power to take the church further along the road, towards its ultimate objective of a completed Reformation.

Prospects for Revival

With amazing stories of church growth being reported from across the globe, some see this as the harbinger of a major move of God in our time. But whether such a move would involve Britain and Europe is another question. For the revival that has been spoken of for the past twenty years or more has yet to come. Anticipation remains high, some saying it has never been higher. Certainly there are encouraging winds that continue to blow, such as the work going on amongst the gypsies and in prisons. Then there is the potential of the *Alpha Course,* which according to *Daily Telegraph* columnist Clifford Longley, suddenly makes the reconversion of England almost believable. [8] But none of this equates to the imminence of revival as it has just been described. The sense of expectation of that requires further explanation.

Just possibly the absence of any significant revival in Europe for the past fifty years is something to do with it. Even the Hebridean revival was about as remote as it was possible to get, and its predecessor in Lowestoft in 1921 was not exactly central. So maybe revival is simply felt to be overdue. Other explanations might have been the rising effect of pre-millennial tension, or the feeling that this is what charismatic renewal really ought to lead to. Alternatively, it may indeed be the Spirit of God who is touching the hearts of His people, that the Europe from which the Reformation emanated would be in the vanguard of the great move He desires to make, and not in the guard's van.

The interpretation, however, that this sense of expectancy therefore means a revival really is just around the corner, should not be so certain. It may well be that God would want it to be so. But it may also be that He does not want to spin the engine of the western church yet again, only to find it still has not been repaired; that it has no more ability by itself to maintain the cycle of compression and combustion it was designed to than when He last tried it.

At the same time, that He is also wanting the western church to look beyond past understandings of revival as the high water mark. To look for more than the short-term revitalising of the church, however welcome that might be. Instead to seek that which will survive long enough to result in a new season of reformation. All of which might explain why He would want to move us beyond a five or a twenty-five year view, into something more like a five hundred year view. Because if it were to be God's desire to release a tidal wave that will exceed all recent high-water marks, then the impact on the western church will go beyond anything we might anticipate, or indeed could even dream of. And despite the present state of the western church, this might well be in the heart of God.

For notwithstanding all his warnings of judgement, Jeremiah also discerned God's never-ending desire to revive the people of Israel far beyond anything they would have ever thought or imagined.

The Lord appeared to us in the past, saying: "I have loved you with an everlasting love; I have drawn you with loving-kindness. I will build you up again and you will be rebuilt, O Virgin Israel. Again you will take up your tambourines and go out to dance with the joyful. Again you will plant vineyards on the hills of Samaria; the farmers will plant them and enjoy their fruit. There will be a day when watch-men cry out on the hills of Ephraim,'Come let us go up to Zion, to the Lord our God.'"

Hear the word of the Lord, O nations; proclaim it in distant coastlands: "He who scattered Israel will gather them and will watch over his flock like a shepherd. For the Lord will ransom Jacob and redeem them from the hand of those stronger than they. They will come and shout for joy on the heights of Zion; they will rejoice in the bounty of the Lord—the corn, the new wine and the oil, the young of the flocks and herds. They will be like a well-watered garden, and they will sorrow no more. Then maidens will dance and be glad, young men and old as well. I will turn their mourning into gladness; I will give them comfort and joy instead of sorrow. I will satisfy the priests with abundance, and my people will be filled with my bounty," declares the Lord.

(Jeremiah 31 v3-6 & v10-14)

God's heart for His people, and His ways with them, remain the same today as then. In every generation, He wants to bring about both the personal renewal and the corporate restoration of His people. Even more importantly, He has exceeding greatness of purpose for the world around. Yet despite His sovereignty, not to speak of His grief over a lost world, He has chosen never to over-ride the free will of His people. Which means He first requires that generation of His people to want to be reformed themselves. Hence Jeremiah's four-fold repetition of the same words:

Reform your ways and your actions ...
(Jeremiah 7 v3, 18 v11, 26 v13 & 35 v15)

He knew that what God wanted to do through His people hinged on their willingness to turn from their evil ways as well as on an unambiguous choice to press forward from there into a lifestyle that was reformed at every level. A profound change first had to happen in them, not just to restore them for their own blessing, but for them to become the blessing to the world God had created them to be. Thus it was that God declared to the people of Judah that following their seventy years in captivity He had plans for them:

... plans to prosper you and not to harm you, plans to give you hope and a future.

(Jeremiah 29 v11)

Yet the story of what happened after their captivity ended reflects how limited their response actually was. Though God's desire had been to prosper them mightily, they only ever found a small measure of that future God had for them. The former blessing that had been on the first Temple never came upon the re-built Temple. The priests were not filled with abundance, nor were the people filled with bounty. They were never greatly used of God to witness to the pagan nations which surrounded them, and little joy was actually found on Zion.

In their experience lie some vital insights regarding both the arrival, and the survival, of revival in any generation. For God's ways do not change. Despite His power to intervene, He only ever works in proportion to the response of His people. First He holds out both prospect and promise, and then He provides an appropriate season of waiting, involving some form of restraint. To the extent that His people respond appropriately as they wait, God blesses; to the extent that they limit their vision or their availability, God withholds. Such may be the explanation of the present position of the western church at this time. For it does not have to be a part of the possible world-wide move of God in our time, however much He might wish it to be. God now has plenty of other churches around the world through which to outwork his purposes. But should the western church be willing to be reformed again in its ways and its actions, it may once more discover a hope and a future. Not only for itself, but also for the nations God has called it to serve.

Chapter Six

Out of Shame

IF THE LAST CENTURY was the only history we had for the western church, we could be forgiven for thinking that the commission to disciple nations was just for the inaugural era of the church. Yet in the story of the sixteenth century Reformation, we have the evidence of what can happen through it to the world beyond. Its effect on politics and government, economics and education, science and art, not to mention religion, demonstrated what the gospel in the hands of a believing church can do to turn the world upside down. Or more accurately, the right way up. If it happened once, it can happen again—providing, that is, the church is free of the entanglements that would otherwise prevent it from pursuing its calling.

Scripture offers various metaphors to describe the identity of the church. It is variously pictured as a body, a bride, a branch, and a building, to name just a few. Each articulates a different aspect of its character. As a body it has unity in diversity. As a bride, it is sustained by love. As a branch it draws strength from the vine it grows from. As a building it stands on its unique foundation and cornerstone: there it stands—it can do no other! Each metaphor emphasises an attribute of the church as it reflects the presence of God's people in the world. Together they reveal a more comprehensive picture of its being. However, being is not the same as doing. Being is needed if doing is to happen, but to appreciate the doing to which the church is called, something more specific than a metaphor is needed.

This we are given in Ephesians 3 v20-21 where Paul speaks of the power of God to do immeasurably more than all we ask or imagine. Whatever human perspective there is to the church, Paul's doxology to God is that "to Him be glory in the church and in Christ Jesus throughout all generations, for ever and ever." Notice how Paul makes no distinction there between the potential of Christ Jesus and that of the church to give glory to God, nor between the potential of one generation of church from another. That statement about the church should truly amaze us. For it means that in any and every way Jesus gave glory to God, so the church of every nation and generation equally has the potential to do so. Which should be the supreme purpose of both its being, and its doing in every age. That a world that was created to give the glory to God but has ceased to do so, should be reclaimed through the mission and the ministry of the church. This brings us to a stark conclusion. The church which does not seek first God's glory and kingdom, ordering its life accordingly is "unfaithful, compromised, undermined, and subverted."[1]

Were it not for the historical evidence of just how far the consequences of the Reformation extended, it would be much easier to spiritualise this principle. Yet what happened in Britain and Europe happened so very tangibly, and so immeasurably more than anything that could have been asked for or imagined. Which means that the proper giving of glory to God cannot be expressed by what happens in a ghetto that meets behind some stained-glass windows once or twice a week. There is no such restriction in the gospel, nor in the potential of the church as God has established it. Instead, if it does not give glory to God out in the world, it is because those who at present constitute its membership are failing to be and to do that which God's people have been called to be and to do, which is to be the salt and light in a tasteless and dark world. For we have been given a gospel that has the power to impact not just the hearts of individuals, but also of nations, and the evidence of history is that the sacred really does have power to sanctify the secular.

The critical question for the present-day western church is therefore how far it is meeting up to its calling. How far is it really fulfilling its potential to do what it could and should be doing in our nation and our generation? Or, putting it the other way round, how far is it falling short of the glory of God? Any assessment is bound to be subjective, but the terrible truth of our time is that it is far easier to find shame in the western church than glory. Numerical decline and general inconsequentiality are just the tip of the iceberg. It is in the nine-tenths under the surface that the real inertia lies. This centres on the compromise of the church with the spirit of the present age. For the church has to a greater or a lesser extent bought into the indulgence of the consumerist age in which we live, and the result is a secularised gospel that is not worth laying our lives down for. Indeed when the church fails to reveal the glory of God sacrificially in and to the world, then, if only by default, the very opposite results. Truth is exchanged for a lie, and glory is exchanged for shame.

We live in a society that places high premium on gratification. Whichever appetite it is, food, sex, material comfort or whatever, the name of the game is to satisfy it.

Furthermore, if it involves bending the rules, so be it. Broadmindedness and tolerance is reckoned to be what is needed, because the only absolute is that there are no absolutes. Should this lead to dysfunctionality, whether in the family, in society or wherever, then the solution is to compensate, and to anaesthetise the pain by taking a holiday from reality; to gratify the cravings of the sinful nature rather than confront them, for it is the pursuit of happiness which matters, whatever the price—and for our western society that price is a catalogue of addiction: not just to drugs, but also to alcohol, nicotine, and caffeine; to gambling and pornography; to work and achievement as well as to success; to overeating and television as well as to exercise and physical conditioning; to clothes and appearance. What defines addiction is the lack of freedom to stop, without transferring from one addiction to another. Hence the drivenness of our addictive, indulgent society that is consumed with its consumerism.

Such is the character of the secular society that has intimidated the western church into compromising the essence of the gospel. It has been seduced into a style of teaching and preaching that more often helps people feel loved and worthwhile, rather than called to self-denial and costly service. Whereas the historic message was that the chief end of man was to glorify God and enjoy Him for ever, nowadays it is made to sound as if the chief end of God is to gratify people. All too easily Christianity and the pursuit of comfort have become intertwined. So Jesus becomes the divine masseur, because healing for our pain matters more than pardon for our sin. Hence, it is not forthright confession we need, so much as therapy to assuage our self-doubts. Here is the point where we lose our grip on the true gospel. For therapy only gives us what we think we need. It takes the gospel to give us what we really need, which is not a change of behaviour, but a change of character. The purpose of the gospel is not to make us happy, but holy; not to provide support, but salvation. It is not about self-realisation, but God-realisation—which means denying ourselves, taking up our cross and following Him. It is therefore not about a package, but a pilgrimage.

Yet in its fear of appearing out of touch with modern times, the western church has accommodated the prevailing culture of relativism. It has relinquished the claim of the Christian gospel to speak of the ultimate absolutes which come alone from the revealed truth of scripture. It therefore presents a message which appears subjective, rather than objective. It loses the perspective of that which is eternal and supernatural, as it imbibes the secular and the natural. It appears to offer just one more alternative truth amongst many and the consequence is that it has lost the ability to speak prophetically into the chaos of modern life. What contrast to the early church that turned the world upside down all because believers confessed that Jesus Christ, and not Caesar, was Lord. Which prevented them, even under the threat of martyrdom, from bowing their knee to Caesar as well as to Jesus. For them, it had to be one or the other and they chose Jesus Christ. [2]

Today, however, our western church cannot give what it does not have. We cannot challenge the secular with the sacred because that involves imparting values we do not really hold in our heart. All our doing is futile until we rediscover the being we were created for. This means breaking free from our acquiescence to secular society, with all its self-indulgences. The freedom of the gospel was not a freedom to indulge the sinful nature (Galatians 5 v13). Such indulgence, which carries with it a continual lust for more, reflects separation from the life of God, and the absence of sensitivity to His ways (Ephesians 4 v19). By contrast, we as church are called to put on the new 'self' created to be like God in true righteousness and holiness, and this involves seeing the whole of life as being *coram Deo*, as lived before God.

The mark of authenticity is in the degree of passion there is to please Him. As against the desire to self-indulge in the sensuality of the culture in which we spend our few brief years. When the church has such passion, the evidence of history is of the amazing power of the gospel to bring glory to God, not only within the church, but also out into the world. Equally, where it does not have such passion, the power of shame quickly takes over. Jeremiah's observation on the waywardness of God's people in his own day was this:

> From our youth shameful gods have consumed the fruits of our fathers' labour—their flocks and herds, their sons and daughters. Let us lie down in our shame, and let our disgrace cover us.
>
> (Jeremiah 3 v24-25)

Times and circumstances have changed dramatically since the days of Jeremiah, but the process and the price of shame has always been the same. It has power to lay people low and eat them up, exactly as it first did to Adam and Eve. When they bought the lie "Did God say ...?" they sold their souls, and with them their identity. As they no longer truly knew who God was, they no longer knew who they themselves were. What happened was much more than the acquisition of guilt. What they also took on was the power of shame. The very last comment on life before the Fall was "the man and the woman were both naked, and they felt no shame" (Genesis 2 v25). Yet through the Fall, the image of God in them was immediately marred and shame entered in. They became spiritually deformed and the immediate consequence of their newly-acquired shame was to cause them to try to evade God. Thus they became the first to discover the principle that as sin expresses man's determination to manage by himself, it is no longer possible to look God in the face.

Though the omniscient God knew what had happened, He still kept His appointment with Adam and Eve, for His love and mercy never ceased. But the power of shame prevented them from doing the same. Hearing the sound of the Lord God as He walked in the garden in the cool of the day, they hid themselves among the trees. When challenged by God, Adam's reply was to say he was afraid. No longer could he bear too much reality, about himself, or about God. Compulsive fear and anxiety had replaced the freedom of love. He felt he had no choice but to run for cover, because he doubted that God was good enough to overwhelm sin with grace. Such is the power of shame. Similarly, if the western church is to come out of its own shame, and to rediscover its God-given ability to reveal His glory to the world, then some very honest admissions are needed. Not only about the place we have reached, but also the road taken to get there. This is no small assignment, given that whenever shame is deep, the tendency to denial is even deeper. Yet only when the western church admits before God its true condition, will we once again be truly available for the glorious purposes He still has for us.

No Hiding Place

To appreciate how much has been lost by the western church, we need to recall the understanding of the gospel that was recovered at the Reformation. As Calvin wrote in the opening chapter of his Institutes,

> Nearly all wisdom we possess, that is to say, true and sound wisdom, consists of two parts: the knowledge of God and of ourselves.

One of his favourite pictures for the estrangement of man from God was the labyrinth, with mankind utterly lost in a maze. He went on to write,

> Hence arises that boundless filthy mire of error wherewith the whole earth was filled and covered. For each man's mind is like a labyrinth, so that it is no wonder that individual nations were drawn aside into various falsehoods; and not only this—but individual men, almost, had their own gods.

Calvin's deep conviction was that only when we see ourselves as we truly are, in our perversity and alienation from God, can we enter fully into the benefits of salvation. In his commentary on Isaiah 53 v6, he put it like this:

> For unless we realise our own helpless misery, we shall never know the remedy which Christ brings, nor come to Him with the fervent love we owe Him ... To know the true flavour of Christ, we must each of us carefully examine ourselves, and each must know himself condemned until he is vindicated by Christ. No one is exempt. The prophet includes *all*. If Christ had not brought help, the whole human race would perish.

Similarly, as we have already considered, it was Luther's perception of the depth of his own sin, measured by the holiness of God rather than by common estimation, that opened his heart to the need for justification by faith. God was not just a concept who could be placed at a distance, as an object of enquiry. He is the living God who meets us in judgement and mercy, who damns us and saves us. *Coram Deo* therefore means that whilst we are always at God's disposal, God is never at ours. "To believe in such a God," said Luther, "is to go down on your knees." It was the phrase "The justice of God" in Romans 1 v17 that had led him to this conviction. It had struck terror into the soul of Luther. All his attempts to satisfy God—his prayers, fastings, vigils, good works—had left him with a wholly disquieted conscience. His mood had swung from despair over his own failures to a simmering rage at God. He once wrote,

> I did not love, indeed I hated, that God who punished sinners; and with a monstrous, silent, if not blaspheming, murmuring I fumed against God.

Yet once Luther grasped what it meant to be declared righteous by God, he felt himself to be reborn and to have gone through open doors into paradise. He was taken out of shame, and into glory and it was this that gave him his almost boundless zeal for reformation. Initially, his heart was for the reformation of western Catholicism, that it too might find the same pathway. By appealing to "the Pope better informed" Luther's hope had been that action from the head of the church might begin a process of healing the decay. The response of the Pope was clear. He did not have any intention of taking even the first step in this direction. Huge numbers of others, however, were more than willing to do so. Or at least to start out in that direction. For what history subsequently records is how over time many who started out on the pathway carved out by the Reformers began to wander off it. Thereby making the edges of Luther's insight into justification by faith, let alone its direction, much less clear for later generations to follow. So it is that the pathway which the Reformers hacked through the jungle of religious confusion is once again heavily overgrown.

Though the Pope's reaction to Luther was not altogether surprising, what requires rather more consideration is why God's people, with the clear-cut pathway of Reformation truth set before them, should have preferred to wander off it back into the spiritual undergrowth. The only explanation is that which Jeremiah discerned,

> The heart is deceitful above all things, and beyond cure.
> Who can understand it?
>
> (Jeremiah 17 v9)

There is much within the human heart that would far rather hide than be healed. Such is the combined effect of pride and shame, even when the way to spiritual freedom is made available. It prefers to scuttle for cover than to find the way out into the light. Perhaps in God's economy it is no coincidence that the Greek word for freedom is *eleutheros*. For it speaks of the price of spiritual freedom as being 'Luthered.' Spiritual freedom requires the honest admission of bondage, a price which many consider too high.

Thus it was in the eighteenth and nineteenth centuries that the Enlightenment provided some much needed cover. Through its pursuit of rationalism, the depth of the analysis of sin discovered by the Reformers could be evaded. The focus was instead put on the affirmation of the essential goodness of human nature. This meant that sin could be defined in a way that was more rationally defensible. The understanding of God was also softened into a form of benevolence, and so the gap between God and man was brought into the reach of the span of reason. The grasp of the need for justification, let alone of its power, was thereby watered down to the point of becoming almost insipid. Which suggested a Jesus who scarcely needed to die for our sins. Furthermore, into this also came 'cheap grace', to use the biting expression coined by Dietrich Bonhoeffer to describe justification without sanctification. That condition where the first vital decision is not followed by the subsequent decisions that make real a costly, continuing journey of discipleship.

All this was a very far cry from the thinking of Joseph Alleine who wrote his *Alarm to the Unconverted* in 1671.[3] In a chapter on the miseries of the unconverted, he wrote this section entitled *The furnace of eternal vengeance is heated ready for you*:

> Hell and destruction open their mouths upon you; they
> gape for you; they groan for you (Isaiah 5 v14), waiting
> as it were with a greedy eye as you stand on the brink.
> If the wrath of men be "as the roaring of a lion" (Prov
> 19 v12), "more heavy than the sand" (Prov 27 v3), what
> is the wrath of the infinite God? If the burning furnace
> heated in Nebuchadnezzar's fiery rage, when he com-
> manded it to be heated seven times hotter, was so fierce
> as to burn up even those that drew near to throw the three
> children in, how hot is that burning of the Almighty's
> fury! Surely this is seventy times seven more fierce.
> What do you think, O man, of being a faggot in hell to
> all eternity? "Can thine heart endure, or can thine hands
> be strong in the days that I shall deal with thee?" (Ezek
> 22 v14). Can you abide the everlasting burnings? Can
> you dwell with consuming fire, when you shall be as a
> glowing iron in hell, and your whole body and soul shall
> be as perfectly possessed by God's burning vengeance
> as the sparkling iron with fire, when heated in the
> fiercest furnace?

We may wince at the style, but if we do it perhaps reflects
how far off the pathway of the Reformers we ourselves might
be. What they recognised was that unless we are impacted
by the shocking aspects of God's wrath against sin, we cannot
appreciate the reality of divine judgement, nor what endless
alienation from God actually means. Only to the extent that
we have realised the fullness of the bad news, can we
comprehend the good news of God's love and mercy.
Otherwise we are vulnerable to the age-old tactic of Satan
which Jeremiah heard the Lord speak of in these terms:

> The prophets are prophesying lies in my name. I have
> not sent them or appointed them or spoken to them.

> They are prophesying to you false visions, divinations, idolatries and the delusions of their own minds.
>
> (Jeremiah 14 v14)

Not only was it in Jeremiah's day that the word spoken by those who purport to be God's ministers may not be His own word. It is simply their delusion about what the truth is, yet it can so easily become other people's delusions as well. A common part of that delusion is that we can hide the truth of our condition from God. But through Jeremiah, this is what He said:

> "Am I only a God nearby" declares the Lord, "and not a God far away? Can anyone hide in secret places so that I cannot see him?" declares the Lord. "Do I not fill heaven and earth?" declares the Lord.
>
> (Jeremiah 23 v23-24)

There is nothing that can be hidden from the omniscient God—however much shame would like to suggest that there is—neither can the reality of judgement be avoided:

> My eyes are on all their ways; they are not hidden from me, nor is their sin concealed from my eyes. I will repay them double for their wickedness and their sin, because they have defiled my land with the lifeless forms of their vile images and have filled my inheritance with their detestable idols.
>
> (Jeremiah 16 v17-18)

Yet under the influence of rationalism and relativism, such delusion can appear to be quite compelling. Insofar as the lie is bought, we increasingly lose sight of just how immense is the covering for sin that God has provided. Its significance, as we perceive it, is drastically diminished. As then is the worth of facing the painful truth about ourselves in order to appropriate what God is making freely available. It is this that leads to the apparent logic of getting off the clear-cut pathway of justification by faith. Imagining it to be a better deal to take to the spiritual undergrowth in the style of Adam and Eve, we make ourselves as comfortable there as we can. The benefit of facing God, we are lured into concluding, is not worth the cost. Much better to sew such modern-day fig leaves as we can find into a do-it-yourself covering for our shame.

Such was Satan's retaliation against the message of the Reformation. The delusion only developed progressively, but once the power of the gospel was devalued, then there was not a gospel for which it was worth counting all things as loss. When that point was reached, there was no longer the sense of being that God intended His church to have. This left a void to be filled, which meant that it was not too hard for Satan to tempt God's people with the things of the world that materialism was producing in ever increasing quantity. For if a sense of being could not be found on the sacred side of the divide, then surely it was legitimate to draw it from some form of compromise with the secular side. So it happened that what was recovered at the Reformation was surrendered piecemeal.

The long-term consequence is that a fair proportion of the membership of the western church now lives out its limited understanding of the gospel amidst a high measure of material comfort, as well as a high measure of exhaustion from what it took to earn the money to pay for the comfort. But the presuppositions that justify all this seem to go largely unquestioned because of what present day indulgences offer—which is the prospect of a slice of instant heaven. The fact that it is a very deluded understanding of heaven on earth seems to be quite by the way.

Worse still, such entanglements hinder the western church's ability to do the things that would impact the nations with the glory of God. Equally they impoverish the sense of being that it takes to truly be salt and light. So instead of where there should be glory, there is the shame that compromise with a fallen world has opened so many different doors to. Were it not for the story of the sixteenth century Reformation, there would be little basis for hope. But our God is the God who never ceases to hold out the vision of restoration, even in the places of the greatest desolation, as He did with Jeremiah in the time of Jerusalem:

> I will heal my people and will let them enjoy abundant peace and security. I will bring Judah and Israel back from captivity and will rebuild them as they were before. I will cleanse them from all the sin they have committed against me and will forgive all their sins of rebellion against me. Then this city will bring me renown, joy, praise and honour before all nations on earth that hear of all the good things I do for it; and they will be in awe and will tremble at the abundant prosperity and peace I provide for it.

> This is what the Lord says: "You say about this place, 'It is a desolate waste, without men or animals.' Yet in the towns of Judah and the streets of Jerusalem that are deserted, inhabited by neither men nor animals, there will be heard once more the sounds of joy and gladness, the voices of bride and bridegroom, and the voices of those who bring thank-offerings to the house of the Lord, saying, 'Give thanks to the Lord Almighty, for the Lord is good; his love endures for ever.' For I will restore the fortunes of the land as they were before," says the Lord.

> (Jeremiah 33 v6-11)

God never ceased to have heart for the restoration of Jerusalem, despite the judgement that had come upon it. We may therefore be sure that He has not ceased to have heart for the restoration of His church, even as it is found in Britain, Europe and the western world today. But the seriousness of its condition suggests a far more radical prescription than just another short-term revival. For the axe has to first go to the roots of its shame if glory is to once again to be seen in it.

Ask for the ancient paths

But who should wield the axe? If the sixteenth century Reformation is anything to go by, it will first need some modern day equivalents of Luther and Calvin to "do something bold for God's sake" to quote one of the last admonitions of another great Reformer, Huldrych Zwingli. For without the tenacious and courageous action of the Reformers, the severance that took place from the shame of the late-medieval church would never have begun. Part of their ability lay in their profound theological learning and their perceptive insight into the culture of their times. Another part lay in their incisive understanding of what was needed if the idols of their day were to be destroyed.

But perhaps the most critical part of their ability was their sense of urgency, through which they motivated ordinary people to respond. To inspire them to sever their dependency on indulgences, and then to allow themselves to be radically touched by the rediscovered gospel. It was ultimately through the mass of ordinary people rather than the few extraordinary reformers that the culture of their society was actually confronted. Even if a new generation of reformers were to come to the fore in today's western church, the question remains whether the ordinary members would be equally responsive. Or this time round, would they favour keeping their indulgences?

Certainly it appears that the modern world has risen up and reached beyond Christianity, evacuating it from its central sphere of influence, and declaring it to be irrelevant to what is now reckoned to be the real world. Such that there is now no way back to that point where Christianity could ever again over-arch the whole of society and culture, defining what was right and wrong, and revealing the nature of true glory. Those days are apparently for ever gone. Yet as G.K. Chesterton put it "Christianity has died many times and risen again; for it has a God who knew the way out of the grave." However much the decimation of the western church may look to be an increasing possibility, the lesson of history is that it is not the only possibility. The story of the sixteenth century Reformation proves that resurrection is not just for individuals after they die, but also for entire nations even before they die. God has placed within every generation of the church the power of resurrection and in the practical demonstration of that truth to the nations is its potential to bring glory to God on earth.

But such conviction is not easy to develop if our only view of the church is what has been seen in the countries of the west during the last century. Indeed it has never been easy for God's people to get hold of the greatness of God's power, or more accurately to be grasped by it, when they are facing decimation or even demise. There is just not sufficient vision of glory to warrant putting aside the superficial comfort that self-indulgence can bring. Which is why we need to hear afresh these words God spoke through Jeremiah:

> This is what the Lord says: "Stand at the crossroads and look; ask for the ancient paths, ask where the good way is, and walk in it, and you will find rest for your souls."
>
> (Jeremiah 6 v16)

Given the particular crossroads the western church has now reached, the greatest wisdom is not likely to be found in too close-up a view of the situation. Instead, it is far more likely to be found in the greater perspective of what Jeremiah calls "the ancient pathways." Nowadays, the best way to find the route of an ancient path is to use aerial photography or even satellite technology. Dense undergrowth might prevent its direction being recognised at ground level, but an overview can make it much easier to see. It is therefore the spiritual equivalent of this seeing from high above that is needed if the ancient pathways of the sixteenth century Reformation are to be recognised by the church's ordinary members.

To follow the Reformation at ground level through each twist and turn is a complex task. Yet, though justice may not be done to every detail of its history, an overview can be appreciated without such ability. What quickly becomes clear is the route the Reformers took to tackle the state of the late medieval church. For it can be defined simply by the connection of two spiritual map references. The first was a penetrating awareness of the nature of God. He is utterly holy, and He created all things to be holy. The other was the equally penetrating awareness of the nature of man, who stands somewhere completely different—at the point of sin.

As it is recognised just how far apart these two points are, even the existence of a pathway from the shame of sin to the glory of holiness can be appreciated for what it is. Let alone for how much it offers those who will renounce their entanglements and indulgences, and begin to walk in it. What the sixteenth century Reformation proved was the possibility not only for individuals, but also for the church, to do so. And on the way, to rediscover not only a lost rest, but also a lost calling. It is surely the recollection of this that we need to seek once more.

Chapter Seven

In to Shema

EVEN SECULAR COMMENTATORS consider that the world is much in need of some form of reformation. In a review of the 20th century, *Time Magazine* commented:

> Theologians have to answer the question of why God allows evil. Rationalists have one almost as difficult: Why doesn't progress make civilisations more civilised?[1]

Such is the dilemma with which the new millennium begins, as the Eastern bloc becomes increasingly post-communist, and the West becomes increasingly post-Christian. For the world it is the problem of our time, but for the church it should be the challenge of our time. First to counter the values of secularism, and secondly to replace them.

From the human viewpoint, this looks like mission impossible. For not only does the West cling to these values, but the Eastern bloc increasingly inclines toward them, despite their manifest failure to make the world a better place. Yet the darkness which needs to be tackled is not so much a presence as an absence of something—the very something which the church alone has in its gift, and also in its calling.

For to follow the call of Christ is to follow the One sent by the God who so loved the world, even as it represented the aggregate of all things earthly. Sent not to condemn it, but to convert it. It is one thing to decry the state of the world, but quite another to save it, as Jesus came to. He came to proclaim the gospel, the nearness of the Kingdom of God, so that His will might be done on earth as it is in heaven. Which, as the sixteenth century Reformation demonstrated, is not mission impossible. Secular value systems that seem to be unassailable can be conquered. They can be overcome by the word of God, just as He promised Jeremiah, saying

> "Is not my word like fire," declares the Lord, "and like a hammer that breaks a rock in pieces?"
>
> (Jeremiah 23 v29)

The good news of the Kingdom was not to be preached as doctrine but as dynamite, as that which could refine and purify with its fire, and smite the walls of every resistance with its blows. It is surely the recovery of this conviction which the western church needs more than anything else if it is to rise to the challenge of our times, and to seize the opportunity. To be truly convinced once more that in this is its gifting and its calling, the outworking of which will not be achieved by resolving the multitude of secondary issues that so preoccupies it—even if that were possible, most of it comes close to fiddling whilst Rome is burning. Instead, the western church needs to be galvanised afresh by Jesus' words about where the roots of the Kingdom of God are to be found, which is in Judaism.

One day a teacher of the law asked Jesus which of all the commandments was the most important.

"The most important one", answered Jesus, "is this: 'Hear, O Israel, the Lord our God, the Lord is one. Love the Lord your God with all your heart and with all your soul and with all your mind and with all your strength.' The second is this: 'Love your neighbour as yourself.' There is no greater command than these."

"Well said, teacher," the man replied. "You are right in saying that God is one and there is no other but him. To love him with all your heart, with all your understanding and with all your strength, and to love your neighbour as yourself is more important than all burnt offerings and sacrifices."

When Jesus saw that he had answered wisely, he said to him, "You are not far from the kingdom of God."

(Mark 12 v28-34)

Nearness to the kingdom of God, according to Jesus, originated in the depths of Jewish tradition. For the greatest commandment, according to Him, grew out of a prayer to be found in Deuteronomy 6 v4-9. Previously it was known to the Jews for many centuries as the *Shema*, which in Hebrew means "Hear..." Jesus then added the words of Leviticus 19 v18, about loving our neighbour as ourselves, which we will consider in the next chapter. But we begin by considering what it might mean, given the vision of a new season of reformation that impacts the nation in which we live, to have a church no longer held back by shame. Instead one which is turned right round, and set free to respond to the continuing call of the Shema.

In Jewish tradition, the four 'alls' of the Shema were declared to be the most crucial and critical response to God. He was to be the sole object of Israel's worship, allegiance and affection. So much so that the command about these words was this:

Impress them on your children. Talk about them when you sit at home and when you walk along the road, when you lie down and get up. Tie them as symbols on your hands and bind them on your foreheads. Write them on the door-frames of your houses and on your gates.

(Deuteronomy 6 v7-9)

The command was taken very literally, being written on small scrolls, and placed in leather containers, called phylacteries, which were bound onto the forehead and left arm, when the Shema was recited twice a day. Jesus condemned the public parading of them as little more than a pride-filled reflection of the letter of the law, rather than the spirit of it (Matthew 23 v5). To do so was to desecrate the challenge and the blessing implicit in it because it was a living blessing. This is why its blessing remains there to this day, not only for our own generation, but also for the blessing of the next generation if we will impress it upon them as well. Indeed, even beyond this that the nation in which we live might be blessed, and enabled to become civilised in a way that all the so-called progress of man has thus far failed to achieve.

"Hear O Israel, the Lord our God is one"

The original Hebrew for "The Lord our God, the Lord is one" is somewhat enigmatic. It consists of four words "Yahweh, our God, Yahweh, one." The essential meaning, however is clear. Israel was to hear this. The object of her worship was not to be diffuse, but single and undivided. It was not a pantheon of gods Israel was to worship, but one definite being whose name is Yahweh. He is Lord alone.

Jesus identified this as the place where the greatest commandment of all began, which was in undivided worship of the Lord. The first Christians, to their great cost, understood this very clearly. Many were martyred, not because they were Christians, but because they would not bow the knee to Caesar as well. It didn't particularly trouble Caesar that they were Christians. The sticking point was that he also required them to bow their knee to him. But for them this was a non-negotiable. There was one Lord, and one Lord alone to whom they could and would bow. The consequence was that many laid down their lives, some in very gruesome circumstances, rather than yield to it. Apparently Caesar had won. Yet quite the opposite happened as a result. It was only a matter of time before the entire Roman empire capitulated and officially became Christian. Such is the power of obedience to the greatest commandment of all to impact the nations.

Which perhaps explains why today we don't see the same impact on society through our witness. Despite our profession, the greater majority of western Christians bow to other gods as well as to the Lord. We simply don't even get off first base with the greatest commandment of all. The real problem is not so much a lack of sanctification (it has been said that there is still enough sin in the greatest saint to ignite the fires of hell), but that of compartmentalising the sacred and the secular, so that the greater majority feel comfortable about being Christians in church, and secularists in the rest of life. We scarcely notice that instead of being in the world but not of it, we are both in it and of it.

This, however, is not something that strikes the western church as particularly wrong. It arises almost unnoticed out of the linking of a personal relationship with Jesus Christ to the privatising of our faith. What results is a façade of Christianity over a secular mind set. We are not penetrated to our core by worship of the one true Lord as we should be, which can easily lead to the view that God is not too bothered with this state of affairs. That He's willing to have an open ear to our every prayer, but equally willing to turn a blind eye whenever it should suit us not to honour Him; that it doesn't trouble Him too much if we worship Him on Sundays, and the gods of secularism and materialism on the other six days of the week; or that on the one day a week when supposedly we do worship Him, we consider the real determinant of its worth to be how personally satisfying we felt the worship to have been.

What all this reflects is how much the thinking of the western church is intertwined with that of the consumerist mind-set, which greatly clouds our ability to see how secular are our values, even for those who would describe themselves as committed Christians. To be discerning about the culture in which we live is never easy. As the Chinese riddle puts it, "If you want to know what water is, why is the fish the last one you ask?" But perhaps an alternative analogy, that of the experience expatriates have when they return to their home country, may help us see where the possibility lies. For after living outside your home country for some time, its distinctive customs are much easier to recognise. Indeed, the longer the time away, the easier it is. For what was once an unquestioned reflex suddenly stands out for what it is. Something you never thought twice about before may now seem quite gauche and inappropriate, and in that moment comes the realisation of how much you were a product of your home culture. So it means the deliberate choice to take some steps out from the secular mind-set, even if we feel, at least for a time, like a fish out of water. But then comes the possibility of seeing how much we were controlled by the spiritual mind-set we originated from or, more precisely, by what controls it.

For it is a mind-set with man at the centre. A mind-set which says that if there is a God, He exists for us, rather than us for Him. But which also echoes the thoughts of Nietzsche that perhaps God is dead. Hence there is no such thing as absolute truth, and no absolute law either. Which means that though others may say that they don't like something I do, they've no objective right to judge it. Everything is relative. So eat, drink and be merry, for tomorrow we die. Such is the all too familiar mind-set that as western Christians we were birthed into and, unless we seek to step back from it, we can have no perspective on how far we are a part of it, on the multitude of tunes we danse to, each representing a vast array of mini-idols that compete for the attention which should be given to the Lord alone. If we don't stand back, it won't stand out, because everyone else is doing it. Moreover, if in our thinking the sacred is split from the secular, it won't feel particularly wrong either. For if the one is kept separate from the other, there is no need for them to inform and challenge each other, either personally or publicly.

But though the dynamics of such delusion are of the moment, there is nothing new here, for the words Jeremiah spoke to the people of Judah are as relevant today as then:

> And when the people ask, "Why has the Lord our God done all this to us?" you will tell them, "As you have forsaken me and served foreign gods in your own land, so now you will serve foreigners in a land not your own."
> Announce this to the house of Jacob and proclaim it in Judah: "Hear this, you foolish and senseless people, who have eyes but do not see, who have ears but do not hear: Should you not fear me?" declares the Lord. "Should you not tremble in my presence?"
>
> (Jeremiah 5 v19-22)

The decline of the western church is therefore not without an explanation. For its worship has not been single and undivided, but has been diluted and diverted as it has incorporated much which is not of the one, true God. Spiritual myopia, if not blindness has resulted, as has much deafness, about where the greatest commandment of all embarks from.

"Love the Lord your God with all your heart"

One of the most liberating aspects of the sixteenth century Reformation, was the rediscovery of the love of God. Calvin particularly asserted that God did not love us because Christ died for us; Christ died for us because God loves us. Indeed he quoted Augustine to show how both the love and the wrath of God are held in juxtaposition.

> Therefore, God loved us even when we practised enmity toward him and committed wickedness. Thus in a marvellous way, he loved us even when he hated us. For he hated us for what we were that he had not made; yet because our wickedness had not entirely consumed his handiwork, he knew how, at the same time, to hate in each one of us what we had made, and to love what he had made.
>
> (Inst. 2.16.4)

So it was that rediscovery was made of the great context of the greatest commandment. What Israel was to hear and live by, as were all of God's people ever after, was this progression. To know God's holiness is to call forth reverence. Reverence should lead to obedience, for obedience is better than sacrifice. Yet the ultimate relationship that God longs for with man is that of love. A love which is to be total, but also voluntary and spontaneous, flowing out of gratitude and devotion. Only as we really grasp what this means can we get to the utter uniqueness of the Christian gospel, which is that "We love because He first loved us" (1 John 4 v19).

Nowadays, the phrase 'loving God with all our heart' must be one of the most overworked and undervalued there is in the entire Christian vocabulary. In an age prone to crass superficiality, what should speak of the highest conceivable commitment often becomes fickle sentimentality. 'Inviting Jesus into our hearts' may therefore be little more than a sentimentalised trivial pursuit, compared with what God has promised. In the words of Jeremiah:

> You will seek me and find me when you seek me with all your heart.

> They will be my people, and I will be their God. I will give them singleness of heart and action, so that they will always fear me for their own good, and for the good of their children after them.

> (Jeremiah 29 v13 & 32 v38-39)

Jeremiah believed that, even for the faithless people he was prophesying to, God's desire was to do a mighty work in their hearts; a work that would have far-reaching consequence across the generations. Providing, that is, it was with singleness of heart, and with an undivided heart, that they sought Him. But Jeremiah was not under any illusions about what that meant. For he also said this:

> The heart is deceitful above all things and beyond cure. Who can understand it? I the Lord search the heart and examine the mind, to reward a man according to his conduct, according to what his deeds deserve.

> (Jeremiah 17 v9-10)

The basic nature of mankind has not changed one iota since Jeremiah uttered these words. Now, as then, the heart of the problem is the problem of the heart, with its profound propensity for self-deception. So unless the preaching of the gospel penetrates to the core of the heart, then all that will result is a commitment that reflects the spirit of the age. The church may pull the wool over its own eyes, convincing itself of its commitment, but God is not deceived. He sees beyond the appearance. We may say "As surely as the Lord lives..."

(Jeremiah 5 v2) but the Lord knows if we are swearing falsely.

The story of Christ's dealing with the rich young ruler has been used to distinguish between much evangelistic preaching of today, and that of Jesus. Indeed, to suggest that many who have 'made decisions' in modern churches and are assured that their sins have been forgiven will be as surprised as Tetzel's customers to hear, "I never knew you. Away from me, you evil doers!" (Matthew 7 v23). Purely because much of our evangelism does not touch what is actually at the core of the heart. What Jesus did was to expose the central love of that young man's heart, and place the question of choice right there, in the area of his love of possessions. Externally, the young man looked so moral and commendable. Apparently he loved God. Internally, it was a very different story. He did not love God with all his heart, and had no intention of doing so either.

The implication is that unless we first preach the true nature of God, when we lead someone to pray after us, we will be praying to the God of glorious holiness, but when he repeats 'God' in his prayer, he will be praying to a divided god, or another god entirely, or even to his 'unknown god'. Unless we have first declared who God truly is, and what His law is, then there will be no wounded conscience, and therefore nothing to bind with gospel bandages. There will have been no opportunity for a truly authentic encounter with the uncompromising love of God, which alone can penetrate, expose and overcome the deceptiveness of the heart.[2]

Without this, there is no real basis for loving the Lord with an undivided heart. Nor for the effective outworking of the greatest commandment of all, through which to bring the nearness of the kingdom of God. A challenge much of the western church needs to hear afresh regarding the content and the style of our personal evangelism if a new season of reformation is to come.

"Love the Lord your God ... with all your soul"

In the book of Deuteronomy, the phrase 'with all your heart and with all your soul and with all your might' is a favourite one. The heart, in Hebrew thinking, was regarded as the seat of the mind and the will, as well as of the whole range of emotions. So these words can just be read as one all-embracing call to love God with unreserved devotion. Yet Jesus challenges us to interpret them in the broader sweep of His teaching. Which takes us into a deeper analysis of the soul of man, and what is required if there is to be no reservation of our commitment to God.

The Reformation doctrine of total depravity does not say that there is no virtue anywhere within us. It does argue however that there is no area within us that is unaffected by the power of sin. To understand how comprehensive a statement this is, we need to remember how complex a being the New Testament declares each of us to be. It describes us as being composed of three parts—a spirit, a soul and a body (1 Thessalonians 5 v23). Commitment of soul, in the sense of the subconscious world view we hold, is therefore not the same as commitment of body, or of spirit. Each of us is a psychosomatic unity, which means that our identity cannot be separated into self-contained parts. What goes on in one part of our being has a measure of effect on every other part. But this does not mean that commitment in one part of us automatically results in the equivalent commitment in another. In this can lie the potential for a grand, and even insidious, delusion. For whether as an unwitting victim, or as a willing perpetrator, this delusion can have serious enough consequences for the soul of an individual. But that is as nothing compared with what it can do in a nation.

One of the most vivid and shocking illustrations of this is the recent story of Rwanda. A country the size of Wales, it is a place of breathtaking beauty, known as the land of a thousand hills. With its gently rolling landscape, it is not without its parallels to parts of Switzerland. Most significantly, it was the home of the East African revival that dated from the 1930's. The country had been evangelised and churches planted. Yet in 1994, Rwanda became a place of fear, death and desolation. A civil war started and unleashed an orgy of terror and violence across the country. Between April 6th and mid-July, genocide occurred. Directed by extremists of the Hutu tribe against the minority Tutsi people and the moderate Hutus, the farmer's working tool, the machete, become known the world over as Rwanda's instrument of death. Out of a nation of seven million people, almost one million were killed, and two million displaced as refugees, first into Tanzania, and then in even larger numbers into Zaire. Amidst all this, huge numbers of families were devastated, women widowed, and many, many thousands of children orphaned or separated from their parents in the chaos which ensued. All in a nation in which around eighty per cent had apparently professed Christ.

Though there is no simple answer for why this happened, it is evident that Rwanda had not been truly permeated with the gospel. Despite the appearance of revival, the soul of the nation, in the sense of the core of its being, had evidently not been transformed. Though it is an extreme picture, it demonstrates how, both for an individual and a nation, it is possible to achieve what looks like an undivided commitment on the surface, whilst masking an unregenerate sub-conscious. The latter being of little consequence until it is forced to show its colours. But in the storm, the true state of the soul is revealed with sharp effect. Then what is beneath the surface, be it rock or sand, is exposed. Whether the house stands, or falls with a great crash, reveals the true nature of its foundation. Such is the intrinsic difference between revival and reformation. Revival can appear to touch the hearts of many, and even to affect the heart of a nation at least for a short period of time. But it requires the deeper work of reformation if the soul of a nation, is to be truly touched.

"Love the Lord your God with all your mind"

The words 'and with all your mind' were an addition Jesus made to the Shema. Quite what He had in His own mind in so doing we are not told. Yet given the struggle over the place of the mind before, during, and since the Reformation of the sixteenth century suggests a measure of foresight. Not only about the potential that lay in mankind loving God with all his mind, but also the downside that follows when mankind does not.

As far back as the eleventh century, Anselm of Canterbury struggled with the balance between faith and reason. "I do not seek to understand in order to believe" said Anselm. "I believe in order to understand." Subsequently, it was the new era of thinking discovered by the Renaissance which was one of the triggers of the Reformation. A vital tool for the outworking of the Reformers' theology was the vigorous exercise of their minds. Their results demonstrated the God-honouring potential for the use of all one's mind, when set in an over-riding love for the Lord. Such that, for example, many of the founders of the Royal Academy of Science were Puritans, who saw their scientific curiosity as an expression of their faith, not a threat to it.

The thinking of the Enlightenment however took the exercise of the mind out from under the Lordship of God. Because fallenness is ultimately the "exchange of the truth of God for a lie" (Romans 1v25), if there is no reference to God, let alone over-riding devotion to Him, then the fundamental thinking of man inevitably becomes fallacious. No longer is truth defined as that which is revealed by God, who alone provides the basis for inquiry and reason. Instead mankind becomes his own source and arbiter of truth. With the advances of the natural world that came from the exercise of the mind, 'enlightened' people, in their view, no longer needed the authority of God. Meaning became rooted in human subjectivity, rather than in relatedness to God, and the existence of the world came to be seen as no more than a bare, independent fact. None of which was helped by the reaction of the church. Often resorting to the use of blind authority, it accelerated the polarisation between faith and reason, and between revelation and human understanding.

So in saying "Just believe", not only did the church impoverish itself, but the kingdom of God was stifled. By declaring Christianity true "because I believe", rather than because God really exists, it effectively endorsed subjectivism. The concept of objective truth, and the distinctiveness of the Christian mind, has become blurred, if not lost. What Christ has done in history, or what He desires to do to impact culture in the future, to push back the results of the fall, has been played down. Sight has been lost of the fact that the gospel is not only to travel around the world horizontally, but also to penetrate culture vertically. Which is why faith, theology, ethics, devotional life and spiritual ministry have become remote from things like science, business, law, politics and art. The lives of Christians have often become compartmentalised as a result, such that Christ's access into our religious compartment is not reflected into that of our work, recreation, politics or family. Because of a lack of critical thinking, this can lead to a form of syncretism which fuses two very different belief systems. Thus it is that the western church has succumbed to secularism as materialism has crept into its values, and humanism into its thinking.[3]

What we therefore need to be 're-minded' of, both as individuals and as church, is the vulnerability that goes with deceived thinking. For the secular frame of reference will not somehow go away if it is ignored for long enough. To the deluded people of Israel, this is what Jeremiah prophesied:

This is what the Lord says: "Do not deceive yourselves, thinking, 'The Babylonians will surely leave us.' They will not! Even if you were to defeat the entire Babylonian army that is attacking you and only wounded men were left in their tents, they would come out and burn this city down."

(Jeremiah 37 v9-10)

Such prophetic warning is as valid today as when it was first given. Unless the western church re-acquires the ability to love the Lord with all its mind, then Babylon will continue to have its day. For the society we live in is no more than the summation of its thinking. It simply reflects the prevailing mind set and the value systems of a world that generally does not think much about the one Lord God. As far back as 1925, J. Gresham Machen stood against the in-rushing tide of humanism, and the anti-intellectual spirit it brought to the church. He wrote:

A revival of the Christian religion, we believe, will deliver mankind from its bondage. Such a revival will not be the work of man, but the work of the Spirit of God. But one of the means which the Spirit will use, we believe, is an awakening of the intellect ... The new Reformation, in other words, will be accompanied by a new Renaissance; and the last thing in the world that we desire to do is to discourage originality or independence of mind.[4]

The reclaiming of the ability throughout the broader body of the church to think with Christian creativity is of the first importance, if the sequence of God's covenant promise to Israel is noted:

> "This is the covenant that I will make with the house of Israel after that time," declares the Lord. "I will put my law in their minds and write it on their hearts. I will be their God, and they will be my people."
>
> (Jeremiah 31 v33)

A sequence proclaimed too little, with a consequence that is felt too much.

"Love the Lord your God ... with all your strength"

> A curse on him who is lax in doing the Lord's work!
>
> (Jeremiah 48 v10)

To those who are given talents for the Lord's work, the question is the same. Will we harness them with all our strength—or will we be lax? "From the one who has been entrusted with much, much more will be asked" (Luke 12 v48). Curse comes to those who are given potential but do not use it. Not only the loss of the potential that was given, but also expulsion into the place of profound regret. Whereas blessing is promised to those who, for the love of the Lord, go to the very limits of their strength, and even beyond into the place of true weakness. His promise to them is to multiply the talents, the strength and the opportunities, and it is through this alone that the kingdom of God is actually advanced. Such is the principle and the promise of scripture (Matthew 25 v14-30). It is also the testimony of the great reformers of every generation.

The story of John Wesley is a notable example. Convinced that at all costs the people of Britain must hear the good news of salvation, it is reckoned that between 1739 and 1791 he prepared and preached over 45,000 sermons. This involved travelling a quarter of a million miles on horseback, often on dangerous and sometimes almost impassable roads. He endured much physical assault, and time after time only narrowly escaped death. Like so many of the Reformers, what Wesley demonstrated was just how great the potential can be for one solitary human being to love God with all his strength. It is said of him that he instilled into the British people a new and Christian conception of courage. He single-handedly demonstrated how God can take the talents of even the most gifted, and multiply them yet further. Thus Wesley was able to think in terms of the most monumental purpose under God—to attack the root cause of Britain's moral decay and to purge the nation's soul. An apparently impossible assignment for any one person, and yet historians still say that the transformation of nineteenth century Britain cannot be explained without an understanding of him. Wesley once asked:

> If sloth and luxury are not, what is the present character of the English nation? It is ungodliness. Ungodliness is our universal, our constant, our peculiar character.

A diagnosis which may apply as much today as then, and may help explain why the western church is not seeing a similar Awakening as happened under Wesley. People may well love God with a limited strength, but certainly not all their strength. Such that the western church is made up of decent people who by and large live with decorum, but not with *coram Deo*. Not with the whole of their lives laid open before God. We are people who often desire to do things right, but who are not necessarily doing the right things. Such that the strength of the church is dissipated on many things, not a few of which are quite secondary. Frenetic busyness can actually mask a laxity in doing the primary work of the Lord which is to bring the kingdom of heaven that much nearer. If our strength is not used to that end, God will not multiply the gift of strength that He has uniquely given through us to the church. Instead it will be taken away, leaving at least our part of the world-wide church lacking in strength to impact, let alone reform, the nations in which it is set.

What apparent contrast to the promise of Jesus in Matthew 16 v18 that the gates of hell would never overcome the church. Often this is taken to mean that though Satan is attacking, the most important thing is not to get anxious. We're to keep our nerve bravely in the assurance that he won't actually break through. Which leads to the notion that Christ's empowering of us is for a glorious defence. That, however, is not what the promise of Jesus was about. It is actually a call to incisive action with all our strength. The gates of a city are meant to prevent the attackers from breaking in, but Jesus' promise is that the gates of hell will not be able to hold out against the advance of God's people. It should therefore inspire the boldest attack against the strongholds of Satan. Christ's empowering of the church is therefore that it may be offensive with all its strength, claiming the ground that the kingdom of God may come in. It is on this vital point of distinction that the effectiveness of the greatest commandment of all hinges.

For in so far as that calling is obeyed, the inward-looking experience of shame is turned into the upward experience of Shema. Instead of hiding from God, we come into hearing Him and into the gift of the reformation experience, which is for God's word to fill the aching void within individuals and nations.

Chapter Eight

And on to your Neighbour

REFORMATION IS ABOUT IMPACTING the world with the redeeming love of God. Which is what Augustine was seeking to expound when he said "Love God and do what you want." Jesus, however, did not make as much favourable assumption about how his words would be interpreted when He responded to the teacher of the law who asked "Of all the commandments, which is the most important?" His answer was in two parts. Firstly, the Shema, plus the extra requirement to love God with all our mind. But then He added that we should also love our neighbour as ourselves. So here, from the lips of our Lord, was the clearest statement of what should be our highest priority, as individuals, as well as church. Unless we obey the full sweep of these words of Jesus, it is not very likely that we will know the fullness of His power within us, let alone through us, to a world which otherwise is lost.

"To love your neighbour as yourself" would have been nothing new to the teacher of the law, being a direct quotation from Leviticus 19 v18. Nor would have been the concept of reducing and summarising the six hundred and thirteen commandments which Jewish tradition considered had been given to Moses. For, despite the practice of expanding the law into myriads of sub-divisions, reduction of the law was also practised by the Jews. Indeed it was even recognised within scripture. For example, in Psalm 15 David reduced the six hundred and thirteen commandments to eleven as he reflected on who it was that may dwell in the sanctuary of God. In Isaiah 33 v15 they are further reduced to six. In Micah 6 v8 they are reduced to three, being "to act justly, and to love mercy, and to walk humbly with your God." In Isaiah 56 v1 the three are reduced to two, being "to maintain justice and do what is right." Finally, in Habbakuk 2 v4 they are reduced to one, namely that "the righteous will live by his faith."

In this perspective, it may seem that Jesus had not said anything new. But in reality, His reply posed a profound challenge not only to the traditional Jews of His day, but indeed to every generation of the Christian church. For His challenge was about where the kingdom of God was truly to be found. In its original setting, loving one's neighbour as oneself referred simply to relationship with one's fellow Jew. It would not have included the Gentile, whom it was quite permissible to hate. Jesus' use of the quotation, however, placed neither qualification nor boundary on its application. His answer to the teacher of the law therefore said this. That the only way love for God can truly be expressed is by our love for our fellow man, without limitation on who that might be. A principle Augustine clearly understood, even if the church soon lost sight of what he really meant.

In Luke's account of the same incident, Jesus went further still in explaining what He meant, using terms which were utterly shocking to His hearers. For in answer to the subsidiary question "And who is my neighbour?" Jesus told the parable of the Good Samaritan (Luke 10 v25-37). In it he debunked the priorities of the priest who passed by the traveller, unsure whether the man was dead. To touch a dead body would have made him unclean for seven days. His turn in the ritual of the Temple would be lost, and this mattered more to him than the pain of a man in need. The Levite refused to take the risk, simply for fear of what he might get implicated in. It was, however, the Samaritan that Jesus pictured as coming to the aid of the traveller. Which to a Jewish hearer was provocative indeed. They had no dealings with the Samaritans, who the Jews regarded as schismatic, if not heretical. In their thinking, Samaritans were not, and could not, be good. If anything, they were irredeemably bad. To get the impact of what Jesus was saying, we might need today to substitute something like "an Irish Republican fell among thieves, and an Ulster Orangeman came and helped him," or "a white colonialist fell among thieves, and a black freedom fighter came to his aid." It was a shocking answer that Jesus gave to the question of "And who is my neighbour?"

Though we don't really know what motivated the teacher of the law to ask Jesus such a leading question, we do know what his conclusion was. Which was that to do what Jesus had said was "more important than all burnt offerings and sacrifices." The response of Jesus was warm and affirming. "You are not far from the kingdom of God" (Mark 12 v34). If our own hearts are also for increasing the nearness of the kingdom of God, we need to understand the implication of these words of Jesus for us as the church of today. Perhaps our present day churchianity, as the modern equivalent of burnt offerings and sacrifices, may put us more in the category of the priest in the parable than we ever realise. For we may be passing by, apparently with the best of intentions, the very situations God's heart most aches for, and in doing, missing the greatest of opportunities for the in-break of the gospel into our society, opportunities with potential not just to transform it, but even to reform it. It may thus be every bit as much to us, as to the people of His day, that Jesus would say, "He who has ears, let him hear" (Matthew 13 v9).

Central to the heart of Jeremiah's prophecy to the people of Judah was a similar challenge:

> This is what the Lord says: "Let not the wise man boast of his wisdom or the strong man boast of his strength or the rich man boast of his riches, but let him who boasts, boast about this: that he understands and knows me, that I am the Lord who exercises kindness, justice and righteousness on earth, for in these I delight," declares the Lord.
>
> (Jeremiah 9 v23-24)

In the Old Testament, justice was not simply a matter of both sides getting a fair hearing. It was about active intervention on behalf of those who could not secure justice for themselves. Kings were therefore to administer justice in this way, because it reflected the character of God the King, and because righteousness and justice were one quality, not two. Which meant that there was no basis for a division between public justice and private morality. It was for this reason that Jeremiah condemned the reign of Shallum, the son of Josiah, who succeeded his father as king of Judah, in these terms:

> "Does it make you a king to have more and more cedar? Did not your father have food and drink? He did what was right and just, so all went well with him. He defended the cause of the poor and the needy, and so all

went well. Is that not what it means to know me?" declares the Lord.

(Jeremiah 22 15-16)

The clear inference was that the blessing of God would only come when love for Him was reflected, not just in love for the neighbour with whom we are on equal terms, but more especially for the one who is not on equal terms with us. Ultimately this must embrace ministry to the weak and the oppressed, for it is this which truly reflects the heart of God. Jeremiah, however, took the principle yet further to a point which was hitherto unprecedented and unique in the ancient world:

> This is what the Lord Almighty, the God of Israel, says to all those I carried into exile from Jerusalem to Babylon: "Build houses and settle down; plant gardens and eat what they produce. Marry and have sons and daughters; find wives for your sons and give your daughters in marriage, so that they too may have sons and daughters. Increase in number there; do not decrease. Also, seek the peace and prosperity of the city to which I have carried you into exile. Pray to the Lord for it, because if it prospers, you too will prosper."

(Jeremiah 29 v4-7)

God's word through Jeremiah to the people of Judah as they were held in exile in Babylon was radical indeed. They were to actively seek and pray for the peace and prosperity of their captors, the very people who were oppressing them, and holding them in a foreign land as captives. Yet though it was against their every instinct, they could not evade the challenge God was giving them. Three times the word *shalom* is used in the original Hebrew. Not to put too fine a point on it, they were to seek nothing less for their captors than the self-same blessing that was intended for them, as God's chosen people. But with this previously unheard of calling, God however added the promise that, if they would obey it, blessing would accrue back to them as well. Thus far did God's heart for righteousness and justice extend.

The promise contained in Jeremiah's prophecy reached on out to a future time as well. A time when One would come to fulfill this calling in ways far beyond anything that the people of Judah could understand there and then:

> "The days are coming," declares the Lord, "when I will raise up to David a righteous Branch, a King who will reign wisely and do what is just and right in the land. In his days Judah will be saved and Israel will live in safety. This is the name by which he will be called: The Lord Our Righteousness."
>
> (Jeremiah 23 v5-6)

In the fulfilment of this prophecy, came the greatest intervention of God's justice this world has seen, or ever will see. Justice which was, however, restorative rather than retributive, for it was the very antithesis of the judgement the world deserved. By giving His Son, God expressed the heart of grace that has always been, and will always be, central within Him. He is the God who dies for His enemies. Furthermore, His desire is to create a people who are similarly characterised by the same love of neighbour. A love which extends even as far as the restoration of enemies.

Jeremiah's prophecy foreshadowed the Sermon on the Mount. In it are to be found the words of the righteous Branch, the king who had come to reign with the wisdom of God. Words which dramatically over-turned the tables of previous understanding. The conventional wisdom of the years had been to love your neighbour and hate your enemy, but here was a new standard. One that was both revelation and revolution. From then on, God's people were to love their enemies, to bless those that curse them, and to do good to those that hate them. Why? To show what it is to be sons of their Father in heaven, not just in principle, but in practice (Matthew 5 v43-45). Because our calling is to tangibly reflect the family likeness, our heart should also be for righteousness and justice that literally knows no limits. For nothing less than this reflects the heart of grace, that as free gift gives to the most undeserving the restoration they most need.

Righteousness and justice as the expression of God's heart of grace are as present in the New Testament as in the Old, but embodied and expressed in the Kingdom of God. Its king is the Lord Our Righteousness. So to live for His kingdom is to live for His righteousness, and for His justice. If His kingdom is to come, and His will be done on earth as it is in heaven, this therefore must include outreach to the poor, the weak, and the oppressed. And it must go further, even as far as loving our enemies, blessing those who curse us, and doing good to those who hurt us.

Inevitably this reign and rule has to begin in personal and private morality. But if the full extent of the greatest commandment is to be obeyed, it cannot end there. Christianity cannot be limited to a private transaction with Jesus. That is not the full gospel, nor the fullness of what Jesus called us to live out. As Chuck Colson points out so eloquently,

> The church is not incidental to the great cosmic struggle for the hearts and souls of modern men and women. It is the instrument God has chosen for that battle—a battle we are called to by virtue of being members of His body. To bring hope and truth to a needy world, *the church must be the church*. [1]

There is no other way that the reformation which alone leads to shalom can be brought to this world. It will only happen in so far as God's chosen channel, the church, makes the fullest expression of the grace of our Lord Jesus Christ in practice. Which means nothing less than loving our neighbour as ourselves, even should they be our oppressor. A calling that is the very antithesis of consumerist Christianity, with its tendency to self-indulgence, rather than to the sacrificial worship and selfless service that Jesus spoke of as our highest priority.

An Open Agenda

However, to address this calling in practice is to expose a largely unresolved item on the agenda of today's church. For the problem is not just a fundamental lack of resolve about truly loving our neighbour as ourselves. That is only the presenting symptom. The real malaise is that there is little agreement within the western church about what it should mean in practice.

One view is that the greatest gift to the poor is to preach the gospel to them. That the greatest starvation is spiritual rather than physical, and that the material condition of the poor stems from their spiritual condition. The bringing in of the kingdom of God will therefore come about through the conversion of their hearts, together with such social action as might follow from that. Those of a dispensationalist view would not agree with this. In their view, the kingdom of God is not present in the age of the church. It will only be established in a future millennium, which means that all attempts to establish justice now are like polishing brass on a sinking ship. The only worthwhile activity is therefore evangelism, which saves souls for a future experience of the kingdom of God. Then there are those who would emphasise social justice as being the very heart of the gospel. For them the primary objective is the changing of society, and that in so far as the impact of God's kingdom can be superimposed on society, in order to Christianise it, it will be this that will actually usher in the kingdom itself.

In between these positions has stood the classic evangelical position that has combined evangelistic preaching with acts of mercy and prophetic social action. As we have already considered, one of the greatest post-Reformation examples was John Wesley. He facilitated a nation in its understanding of what a comprehensive answer to the greatest commandment meant in practice. Primarily remembered as an evangelist, the gospel he preached nonetheless inspired people to take up social causes in the name of Christ. To such an extent that historians have attributed to his influence, more than any one else's, the sparing of Britain from a revolution such as France endured. The nineteenth century saw a continued connection between evangelism and social action, of which the abolition of slavery was just one consequence. Yet the story of the twentieth century has been very different.

A number of reasons have been suggested for what has been called 'The Great Reversal'. Firstly, the fight against liberalism, which at the turn of the century was seeping into the churches of Europe and America. Evangelicals felt they had to vindicate the fundamentals of the faith, and this left little time for social concerns. Secondly, they reacted against the emergence of the so-called social gospel, with its emphasis not on getting individuals into heaven, but of transforming life on earth into the harmony of heaven. Thirdly, there was the impact of widespread disillusion and pessimism at the end of the First World War. Man and his society seemed to be irreformable. Fourthly, there was the spread of the dispensationalist view of the kingdom of God, which holds that the world can and will only get worse until the return of Christ. Fifthly, there was the spread of Christianity amongst middle-class people, whose values were generally conservative and orientated toward maintaining the status quo, with little sensitivity to the needs of the poor.[2]

It was a powerful cocktail of reasons that variously reduced and fragmented the evangelical understanding of loving our neighbour as ourselves. Yet though it arose out of the circumstances prevailing at the beginning of the twentieth century, the possibility for it to happen may have had its origins in the Reformation itself. Or more accurately, in the incompleteness of what happened at the Reformation.

When Luther made his great discovery about justification by faith, it was at that stage nothing more than his finding of an answer to a personal quest. His objective was not the establishment of a grand plan through which to reform the church. Let alone to release the sequence of events that were to have such impact on the nations. Little did this solitary monk realise he was setting in motion events that would shape the character of western civilisation for centuries to come. He was simply agonising over the justice of God. Manifestly the church with its hierarchies and religious systems could not give him a clear-cut answer to a straightforward question. It was this that provoked the depth of searching the eventually brought him to his great 'back to the text' breakthrough that righteousness was "from first to last, by faith" (Romans 1 v17). In fact what Luther grasped from Paul was only what Paul had apparently grasped from his own exercise of back to the text, re-discovering Habakkuk's reduction of the law, that "the righteous will live by his faith" (Habakkuk 2 v4).

Luther had no perception of the significance of what he was doing—that he was laying the cornerstone of the sixteenth century Reformation. Little did he realise that not only was he choosing the location of its site, but that he was also laying the first part of the foundation, on which so much else was later to be built. In doing so, he was selecting the formative, if not the definitive theological angle against which everything else was to be built. For the process involved in constructing the theology of the Reformation was not dissimilar to what happens in the construction of a building. First a site is chosen. Next the preferred view from that site is decided upon, often involving the selection of one outlook as against another. This then determines the direction of the main windows, and from that the orientation of all the other features of the building. When the time for construction comes, the cornerstone of the foundation is placed to reflect the selected use of the site. Which is exactly what happened as the result of Luther's theological agonising. However little he realised what he was doing, what he did was to choose not only the site on which the theology of the Reformation would be built, but also the very particular direction its outlook would have.

The cornerstone of justification by faith defined the whole subsequent building process the Reformers became involved in. As they sought to reclaim the truth of the Early Church, they looked out for it primarily in this specific and distinctive direction. Had Luther chosen a different angle for his cornerstone, which more fully encompassed grace as well as faith, it is not impossible that the subsequent story might have had a different emphasis. For even on the exact same site where the theology of the Reformation came to be built, it would have been equally possible for its primary outlook to have been given a somewhat different orientation. Especially if Luther's personal breakthrough had instead majored on, for example, Romans 3 v24 which speaks of being "justified freely by his grace through the redemption that came by Jesus Christ." Or on Romans 5 v2 which speaks of gaining "access by faith into this grace in which we now stand."

Had grace received as much, or even more, prominence as faith in Luther's summary of what it takes to be saved, the theology of the Reformation may have been given a somewhat different emphasis. So too may the whole momentous chain of events that were to follow from it. As it reaches us today, a much firmer foundation may have been provided for understanding what Jesus really meant about loving our neighbour as ourselves, even should that neighbour be an enemy. An understanding which might not have caved in so easily under the pressures of the twentieth century.

Luther himself was not unaware of the outlook of grace being very close to that of faith. "If you have a true faith that Christ is your Saviour" he once wrote, "then at once you have a gracious God, for faith leads you in and opens up God's heart and will, that you should see pure grace and overwhelming love."[3] But what should equally be remembered was his description of the book of James as "an epistle of straw ... that mangles the scriptures." For him, the emphasis that James put on "faith by itself, if it is not accompanied by action, is dead" (2 v17) warranted its relegation to the end of his German translation of the New Testament. Indeed, he came close to declaring it as secondary scripture, because justification by faith alone had in his view to be the principal orientation. In being so adamant about it, Luther gave a far greater foundation for the fulfilling of the first part of Jesus' definition of the greatest commandment than of the second. For the exercise of faith leads much more to the touching of the heart, mind and soul than to a practical loving of one's neighbour as oneself. But just as it takes one hand to wash the other, both were actually needed to be equally reclaimed for a comprehensive Reformation to have taken place.

Certainly there had been some great examples between the time of the Early Church and the Reformation of those who grasped the connection between faith and grace, and also applied it. Basil of Caesarea (330-379) was a notable example. He established orphanages, schools, poorhouses, and hostels for poor travellers, caring for the thousands of poor and neglected who came to his city. He is best known for developing the first fully staffed hospitals. He said, "A man who has two coats or two pairs of shoes, when his neighbour has none, evidences a lack of grace in his life. The re-distribution of wealth is not the point. The revealing of faith is the point."

John Chrysostom (347-407) was called 'the golden-mouthed orator.' He is considered one of the greatest preachers in the history of the church. Yet he devoted more time and energy to serving the poor than to preaching. He established many Christian charities, hospices, and hospitals for the destitute. He said, "The essence of the Gospel is not concern for the poor, but it certainly provokes that concern. In fact, without that concern, the essence of the Gospel surely has not been grasped."

Augustine of Hippo (354-430) is probably the greatest theologian in the history of the church. Yet he also had a profound impact on the economy of North Africa through the development of works of charity in thirteen cities. Gregory the Great (540-604) co-ordinated efforts to help victims of war, pestilence and famine throughout the time of his ministry. He gave from his personal income, and he also donated large amounts from the church. Bernard of Clairvaux (1090-1153) is best known as the father of one of the greatest monastic movements in church history, which resulted in many people coming to Christ. He also established a network of hostels, hospices, and hospitals which have survived to the present day.

John Wycliffe (1329-1384) is best known for his English translation of the New Testament, which revived interest in the Bible, and helped lead to the Reformation. He also led a grass-roots movement of lay preachers and relief workers who ministered to the poor. Jan Hus (1374-1415) was a dynamic preacher, evangelist and reformer who helped pave the way for Luther. He also organised an army of workers for emergency relief when Central Europe was struggling under war, famine, poverty, and moral degradation. He won the hearts of people through his preaching and his good works. He said, "Doubt must be cast on fruitless lives. Profession of faith must be followed by deeds of charity, otherwise that profession is false."[4]

But despite such fine examples of those who had grasped the connection between grace and faith, these were the exceptions. By the time of the sixteenth century Reformation, for the greater part of the church, faith had become far removed from anything to do with the person and work of Jesus Christ. Instead, it was submitted to the overwhelmingly superior authority of the church. So much so, that the church was the exclusive purveyor of its home-spun substitute for grace, which it sold on the terms it chose. To increase the pressure to buy its indulgences, the priests depicted in horrifying terms the fire in which men would be purified from the sins that could not be expiated on earth. No means were spared to fill the mind with terror, which explains why the Tariff of Indulgences went through more than forty editions. It is said that even the least delicate ears would be offended by an enumeration of the horrors it contained. Incest, if not detected, was to cost five groats; and six if it was known. There was a stated price for murder, infanticide, adultery, perjury, burglary and so on. Who, it was questioned, could refuse the ransom which, as it fell into the treasury of Rome, would redeem the soul from such torments? It was this far that the church prior to the Reformation was from any true understanding of either faith or grace.

The extent of what Luther achieved, however inconceivable to him as he hammered his notice onto the church door in Wittenberg, is marvellously described in the D'Aubigné's *History of the Reformation*. He writes:

> Primitive Christianity and the Reformation are the two greatest revolutions in history. They are one and the same revolution, brought about at different epochs and under different circumstances. Although not alike in their secondary features, they are identical in their primary and chief characteristics. One is a repetition of the other. The former put an end to the old order; the latter began the new: between them lie the Middle Ages. One is the parent of the other; and although the daughter may in some instances bear marks of inferiority, she has characteristics that are peculiarly her own.

Despite all that did happen, lack of clarity about what Jesus meant for us to love our neighbour as ourselves, even should our neighbour be our enemy, is a critical part of that continuing inferiority and peculiarity. If there is to be a new season of reformation, this surely cannot be left as open agenda.

True Grace

An exposé of what needs to be tackled in today's western church is given through the absence of what is spoken of in Acts 4 v32-33. The picture there is of all the believers being of one heart and mind. In that context, no-one claimed any of his possessions to be their own, but they shared everything they had. As they loved their neighbour as themselves, we are told that three things resulted. Firstly, there was not a needy person among them. Secondly, the apostles experienced great power as they continued to testify to the resurrection of the Lord Jesus. Thirdly, much grace was with them all.

Despite the notable exceptions that followed the Reformation as well as preceded it, such an understanding of church has never been fully reclaimed. During the period of the Reformers, the task in hand was far more to do with self-preservation, consolidation and instruction than social witness. Calvin's Geneva for example, though a high water mark for a focused expression of the kingdom of God, was characterised more by stringency than grace. To call Calvin 'the great dictator' and to describe Geneva under Calvin as 'more like Jerusalem under the high priests than the heavenly city' is reckoned to be overstatement. Yet the consistories he set up to show individuals the errors of their ways, and his excommunication of the wayward, are facts of history. Certainly this previously corrupt and dirty city was dramatically reformed within one generation. Prosperity did indeed result from the work ethic which flowed from the values of the Reformation, and need was quickly eliminated. To such extent that the city was enabled to become a significant place of refuge for the persecuted. But even Geneva under Calvin was still a long way from the practice of the early Christians in the putting of all their goods at the disposal of one another, and of the kingdom. Despite the glory of the story, it was not all true grace.

Certainly it has to be admitted that, as with the construction of a house, the Reformation could not have been built with its principal outlook going in two directions at once. It had to major on one view, or another. Had Luther's primary emphasis been on grace rather than on faith, then the subsequent story may have had a rather different feel. Other things may have been accomplished, but at the price of an alternative inferiority and peculiarity. However whilst all this can be debated, the facts remain. The western church as it enters the third millennium is not of one heart and mind. Nor does it generally have great power in testifying to the resurrection of the Lord Jesus. Neither is much grace with us all.

Manifestly something very fundamental is missing. It is evidenced in many ways, but perhaps the leading indicator is this. We have, in the western church, only the most minimal grasp of just how exceedingly radical is the call of Jesus to gracious action. Until this aspect of the life of the Early church has been reclaimed, we are simply passing by on the other side. We are not only missing the situations God's heart aches for the most, but also the opportunities for the greatest in-break of the gospel. The work of Reformation is therefore yet to be completed. The full gospel has not been reclaimed, let alone the fullness of its power to impact the nations. Instead we have an all too easy acquiescence to the values of a thoroughly secularised culture, that puts rather more premium on personal comfort and self-indulgence than on loving one's neighbour.

Just as the sixteenth century Reformation broke the grip of Tetzel's indulgences, so the self-indulgence that grips today's church also needs to be broken. But whereas the 'back to the text' breakthrough five hundred years ago was the rediscovery of justification 'by faith', perhaps it is the meaning of being justified 'freely through grace' that now needs to be rediscovered. Which is not just about the acquisition of a greater understanding of grace as it is commonly defined, namely the unmerited favour of God. Such a view of grace is all too easily consumed upon ourselves. What needs to be widely rediscovered is that appreciation of grace, which, as the fiery slave trader John Newton realised, is so amazing that it turns our hearts to defend the poor and needy. Grace which both causes and enables us to do that which would otherwise run clean contrary to natural inclination. Grace which, as one description puts it, is the empowering presence of God to enable us to be what He wants us to be, and do what He wants us to do—which is to love our neighbour as ourselves. It is this, above all things, which is needed if a generally ungracious world is to be impacted by the kingdom of God.

The picture of the Early Church in the fourth chapter of Acts provides the primal case study of what happens when such grace is present. There we see the first Christians doing the exact opposite of getting their personal needs met. Their heart was simply to reflect the ministry of the Word become flesh, who had come from the Father, full of grace and truth (John 1 v14). They had seen Him not only preach the good news that the kingdom of God was near, but also physically minister to the poor and needy. Not only did He preach forgiveness of sins, but He also healed the sick and fed the hungry. Through this, they had come to understand the meaning of the incarnation. The Father had not only sent the Word, He had physically given flesh. Each was embodied in the other as God expressed His love for a world which was at enmity with Him. The ministry of Jesus, which they were called to continue, was therefore clear. Grace could not be expressed if truth was not proclaimed, and truth could not be proclaimed if grace was not expressed.

It was not long, however, before the Early Church had to work this out in the face of rapidly escalating hostility. Yet it was these circumstances which provided the greatest opportunity to demonstrate the kingdom of God. For it was the manner in which they faced their oppressors which had such effect. It was this, if anything, which brought about the spectacular expansion of Christianity that was to so impact western civilisation for the next two thousand years. The aim of the Early Church, however, never was to correct the ills of society. It was simply to live out the things God delights in, which are kindness, justice and righteousness; to love one's enemies, and even to pray shalom upon them; and to incarnate grace and truth which testifies to the resurrection of the Lord Jesus Christ personally. As they did this, the kingdom of God broke in. The world was impacted in ways beyond anything they could ever have thought or imagined, let alone orchestrated. Yet it happened purely as a by-product of the in-break of the kingdom of God, and not as a primary objective. For this was the full gospel, not just the social gospel. It was to this that Augustine was referring in another of his cryptic precepts when he said, "Preach the Gospel everywhere. Only use words when necessary."

Such would appear to be the process of reformation upon which God puts His blessing, as Luther and his fellow Reformers were also to discover, even if only in an inferior way. That where the spiritual justice of the kingdom of God is authentically sought, it will inevitably have social and political consequences. For grace and truth cannot just be expressed with words. They have to become flesh if the glory of the Lord is to be seen.

Chapter Nine

The Price of More Reformation

DESPITE THE INCALCULABLE BENEFITS of the sixteenth century Reformation, its cost was immense in the schisms and even the wars that it led to. Yet on that critical day in Wittenburg, October 31st 1517, Luther apparently had not the slightest inkling of either the costs or the benefits that were to follow from his actions. What he did, he did quite unwittingly! Action needed to be taken, and he had the material to do it with. At that time, nailing theses to a church door was the normal way to launch a debate. There was a plethora of issues he could have raised about the state of the church, but he chose to centre on just one—the selling of indulgences. It was a bold step, but that is all it was. There is no evidence that he had a huge master plan, of which this was the first step, to bring about something to be called the

Reformation, let alone to bring about another thing to be called Protestantism. For Luther was not a strategist who worked out his moves in advance. All he did was to keep on responding to the blaze he had somewhat unintentionally ignited, but which, in the hands of God, was enough to change the course of western history. The human cost, however, should not be overlooked.

Compared with modern management techniques, Luther's approach would not look like the way to change anything much, let alone the church or a nation. Today's conventional wisdom says that goals have to be specified, and then action plans designed that those goals may be reached. Strategy, tactics, aims and objectives are what it takes, because the laws of physics prove that every action has an equal and opposite reaction. So we have to define the reaction we want, and then work back to the action that means in practice. Such is the way Enlightenment thinking works, and there is no denying the material results it has brought to this world. But at our peril we forget that lasting spiritual results are not achieved in the same way.

For it was neither how the Early Church turned the world upside down, nor how Luther and the other Reformers achieved what they did. The explanation is simple. It is God alone who has the power to touch the fundamental state of a church, or a nation. As the story of Jeremiah's visit to the house of the potter so graphically reminds us.

> This is the word that came to Jeremiah from the Lord: "Go down to the potter's house, and there I will give you my message." So I went down to the potter's house, and I saw him working at the wheel. But the pot he was shaping from the clay was marred in his hands; so the potter formed it into another pot, shaping it as seemed best to him.
> Then the word of the Lord came to me: "O house of Israel, can I not do with you as the potter does?" declares the Lord.

"Like clay in the hand of the potter, so are you in my hand, O house of Israel. If at any time I announce that a nation or kingdom is to be uprooted, torn down and destroyed, and if that nation I warned repents of its evil, then I will relent and not inflict on it the disaster I had planned. And if at another time I announce that a nation or a kingdom is to be built up and planted, and if it does evil in my sight and does not obey me, then I will reconsider the good I had intended to do for it."

(Jeremiah 18 v1-10)

The power of lasting reformation is entirely in the hands of God, and it is the grandest of delusions to think otherwise. Sovereignly and omnipotently, God can reshape a nation or a church as and when He chooses, for He is the Potter. What we are powerless to accomplish, He can do with irresistible ease. The only contribution the church can make is to be willing to pay the cost of being reformed into a new shape that will bring greater glory to Him. This is what Luther facilitated and to which the people, even if not the hierarchy, of the church responded. We will never know what disaster Luther's uncalculated actions averted from falling upon the church of his day. Let alone what the consequences would have been for us today had he not done what he did. All we do know is that God reshaped the church and the nations in ways far beyond Luther's wildest dream as he hammered his ninety-five theses to that church door, which even the most expansionist plans of man would never have dared to aim for, let alone achieve.

The present state of the western church should not therefore prevent us from believing for what is possible, even if it may not look too probable. But it will be the plans of God, rather than the plans of man, that will bring it about. In an age that places much confidence in its strategic planning, the warning God gave through Jeremiah is very pertinent:

> Now therefore say to the people of Judah and those living in Jerusalem, "This is what the Lord says: Look! I am preparing a disaster for you and devising a plan against you. So turn from your evil ways, each one of you, and reform your ways and your actions."
> But they will reply, "It's no use. We will continue with our own plans..."
>
> (Jeremiah 18 v11-12)

So the challenge to the western church is how willing it is to become clay in the hands of a potter, relinquishing its rights to its shape. Or whether it will be more like the clay pot of Isaiah 29 v16 that argues with the Potter as to who knows best. We have no ability, let alone any right, to tell God what a new season of reformation should involve. All we know is that it will not be without its cost, and the more consequential the change, the greater the cost is likely to be. The only choice is whether the individuals of the church, and indeed the institutions of the church, will be willing to pay the price.

To demonstrate the cost of what more reformation could possibly involve, three inter-related examples are offered. They are given merely by way of illustration, rather than as prescription, purely to give the feeling of the cost rather than to name the price. But hopefully they will suffice to suggest the types of re-shaping that might be involved as well as the commitment needed to embrace them. On such may well hinge whether the next generation seizes or loses the opportunity of reformation.

Illustration 1:
A reformed attitude to the Jews

One of the breakthroughs of the Reformation that almost happened, but never did, was the reforming of the Church's attitude to the Jews. Luther came very close to reversing the legacy of persecution that stemmed from the first Crusade.

During it, many Jewish communities in France, Germany and Jerusalem were massacred. Then followed the Church's decree in 1215 that all Jews should wear a badge of shame. Jews were increasingly segregated apartheid style, and became the outcasts of mediaeval Europe. The Church demonised the Jews, and hundreds of thousands died as a result. Initially, Luther attacked the Church with these words:

> They have dealt with the Jews as though they were dogs and not human beings. They have done nothing for them but curse them and seize their wealth. I would advise and beg everybody to deal kindly with the Jews and instruct them in the Scriptures. In such a case we could expect them to come over to us ... we must receive them kindly and allow them to compete with us in earning a livelihood ... and if some remain obstinate, what of it?[1]

Indeed, when Luther was dubbed by the Vatican as a 'half-Jew' he accepted that designation with these words:

> They [the Jews] are blood-brothers of our Lord; if it were proper to boast of flesh and blood, the Jews belong to Christ more than we. I beg, therefore, my dear Papists, if you become tired of abusing me as a heretic, that you begin to revile me as a Jew.

Yet, when the Jews failed to respond to Luther's invitation and preferred to stay in Judaism, he turned bitterly against them, saying:

> Burn their synagogues and schools; what will not burn, bury with earth, that neither stone nor rubbish remain. In like manner break into and destroy their homes. Take away their prayer-books and Talmuds, in which there is nothing but godlessness, lies, cursing and swearing. Forbid their Rabbis to teach, on pain of life or limb.[2]

In his defence it may be said that Luther was already a sick man, and was also battling at the time with the German peasants who were using Protestantism for their own ends, to free themselves from serfdom. But for all the positive outworking of God's plans that Luther's actions facilitated, in this respect it was the exact opposite. Such that when Hitler claimed to a Roman Catholic bishop that in persecuting the Jews, he was simply continuing what the Church had done for sixteen centuries, it is reckoned this was largely true. Had Luther not reversed his position, it is not impossible that the anti-Semitism of the twentieth century might not have happened as it did.

If the western church is to know a new season of God's blessing, then this could be one of the first areas of unfinished reformation God will call it to face. The starting point for which will be to repent over its lost understanding of God's promise to Abraham in Genesis 12 v2-3 that "I will make you into a great nation, and I will bless you; I will make your name great, and you will be a blessing. I will bless those who bless you, and whoever curses you, I will curse; and all peoples on earth will be blessed through you." Even the construction of scripture highlights the significance of these words to Abraham. Scripture contains just two chapters on creation, and only nine more to cover the first two thousand years or so of history. But then come fourteen chapters on the life of Abraham, followed by nine hundred and twenty nine covering Israel's birth through to the coming of the Messiah. Even the genealogies of the gospels show how Jesus came from the lineage of David, who was descended from Abraham. As if this is not enough, there are also the repeated affirmations of Israel's pivotal role in the blessing of the nations, such as in these words of Jeremiah:

"If you will return, O Israel, return to me," declares the Lord. "If you put your detestable idols out of my sight and

no longer go astray, and if in a truthful, just and righteous way you swear, 'As surely as the Lord lives,' then
the nations will be blessed by him and in him they will
glory."

(Jeremiah 4 v1-2)

These words suggest that until the church is reformed in its
attitude to Jewish people, to enable them to know the Lord,
it will be under a cloud of curse rather than raised up into
blessing. Furthermore it will have failed in its part to enable
the world to receive the blessing that God, in His sovereignty,
has chosen to minister to the world exclusively through the
Jewish people.

One of the ways the church has justified its attitude to the
Jews is by arguing a theology of replacement, claiming that
it has become the 'new Israel'. But there is much danger in
such an argument, because it ignores the greater sweep of
scripture. Indeed only one verse in the entire New Testament,
Galatians 6 v16, can even be construed in this way.
Furthermore, though the prophets repeatedly speak out
denunciation of Israel's sin, they regularly follow it with the
promise of restoration. So, for example, all the complaints
of Jeremiah in 3v19—5v17 are followed by the promise

"Yet even in those days," declares the Lord, "I will not
destroy you completely."

(Jeremiah 5 v18)

And the denunciations of Jeremiah in chapters 7 to 12 v13
are followed by these words:

As for all my wicked neighbours who seize the inheritance I gave to my people Israel, I will uproot them from
their lands and I will uproot the house of Judah from
among them. But after I uproot them, I will again have
compassion, and will bring each of them back to his
own inheritance and his own country.

(Jeremiah 12 v14-15)

Underlying these words of prophecy are two fundamental principles. Firstly, that the Lord is committed to vindicating His name. Secondly, as Paul puts it in Romans 11 v29, "God's gifts and His call are irrevocable." Or as Jeremiah expresses it:

> This is what the Lord says, he who appoints the sun to shine by day, who decrees the moon and the stars to shine by night, who stirs up the sea so that its waves roar—the Lord Almighty is his name: "Only if these decrees vanish from my sight" declares the Lord, "will the descendants of Israel ever cease to be a nation before me ... Only if the heavens above can be measured and the foundations of the earth below be searched out will I reject all the descendants of Israel because of all they have done," declares the Lord.
>
> (Jeremiah 31 v35-37)

The very greatest of thanks should be given that this is the case, for if God could break His promise to Israel, what confidence could we in the western church of today have that God would keep His promise to us? How thankful we should be that God has not given up on Israel (Romans 11 v1). And how excited we should be that "because of their transgression, salvation has come to the Gentiles to make Israel envious. But if their transgression means riches for the world, and their loss means riches for the Gentiles, how much greater riches will their fullness bring!" (Romans 11 v11-12). If we value the theology of Romans for releasing the sixteenth century Reformation, then should we not equally value the teaching of chapters 9-11 as possible material for a future season of Reformation?

Amongst the circumstantial evidence of the truth of this is the persistent survival of the Jewish people as a distinct ethnic body. Despite fearsome rejection and persecution, they have not only survived, but have continued to draw the world's attention. Not only has this century witnessed the murder of five million of them, but it has also seen fifty years of the modern state of Israel. After nearly two thousand years of exile, it takes some courage to dismiss this as just a fluke of history. Jeremiah is just one of many prophets who spoke of the return of a widely scattered Israel as a significant milestone in salvation history:

> "However, the days are coming" declares the Lord, "when men will no longer say, 'As surely as the Lord lives, who brought the Israelites up out of Egypt,' but they will say, 'As surely as the Lord lives, who brought the Israelites up out of the land of the north and out of all the countries where he had banished them.' For I will restore them to the land I gave to their forefathers.'"
>
> (Jeremiah 16 v14-15)

> See, I will bring them from the land of the north and gather them from the ends of the earth ...
>
> (Jeremiah 31 v8)

Though the return from the exile in Babylon matched some of the prophecies, by no means did it fulfill all those which spoke of a worldwide return. Caution also has to be exercised about too fundamentalist an interpretation of what we have seen in the historic land of Israel these past fifty years. Currently, all that is there is a modern secular state, not especially notable for its moral or spiritual qualities. It cannot be described as the completion of these unfulfilled prophecies. Yet even its coming into existence, let alone its survival for over half a century, not to mention its centrality on the political stage of the world, should challenge the church regarding its rejection of the Jewish people. It may well be that the Biblical promises for Israel are ultimately more for spiritual than physical fulfilment. As the Puritans put it, they may be fulfillled either in the letter or in the better. But the return of the Jewish people in our time to their historic land at the very least affirms the lasting validity of

God's promises to them. Furthermore, it underscores the fullness of the promise He still holds out to the world through them.

To this must be added the recent, spectacular rise of Messianic Judaism. For the first time since the early Christian generations, there is a statistically significant proportion of Jews who accept Jesus as Messiah without abandoning their Jewishness. Of the 14,785,000 people in the world who consider themselves Jews, research indicates that 132,000, or almost 1%, see Jesus as the Messiah.[3] We can only speculate what the impact upon the world will be if the rate of conversions amongst the Jews continues to rise yet more dramatically still. But what has happened already with the Jewish people might well be considered another of those conjunctions of circumstance that indicate the possibility of a new season of reformation. For the greater proportion have come to know the Lord since Jerusalem was recaptured in 1967. It therefore challenges the church to be reformed in its attitude to the unique place of the Jewish people in the plan of God. For though we may struggle with the fullness of what this means, in it is to be found the glory of God (Romans 11 v33-36). Which means owning both the debt and the responsibility the Church has to the Jewish people, however high the price of doing that might be.

Illustration 2:
A reformed attitude to unity

A second area of consideration for what a new season of reformation might involve is that of unity, for it spotlights another promise of immense blessing to the nations if the church will obey its calling. In Jesus' last words before His arrest He prayed for all believers like this. "May they be brought to complete unity to let the world know that you sent me and have loved them even as you have loved me". (John

17 v23). Jesus' urgency in prayer revealed His belief that there would be a profound correlation between the unity of the believers, and their potential to impact the world. In fact the complete unity of the church is one thing there has been little disagreement about ever since—at least in principle! The Nicene Creed, drawn up in AD 381, spoke of faith in "one holy, catholic and apostolic Church." Unfortunately creeds don't explain how faith should be expressed in practice, and the sixteenth century Reformation did little to resolve the problem. Indeed, in many senses it only made matters a great deal worse.

For far beyond causing the basic split from Rome, the Reformation also triggered the rampant denominationalism that has characterised the Protestant church ever since. Effectively it was the watershed from which flowed most of the estimated 25,000 different denominations that now exist around the world.[4] Diversity within the church is not necessarily wrong, for God has built into the created order an almost incomprehensible diversity. But whilst diversity is one thing, disunity is quite another. The minimal impact on the world of our divided western church is prima-facie evidence of the basic rule of warfare 'divide and conquer.' Allowing itself to become so divided has weakened the church's ability to stand where it is, let alone to move forward with the gospel. By contrast stands the impact on the world of the Early Church in which "all the believers were one in heart and mind" (Acts 4 v32). The present fragmented and divided Christianity is ultimately a scandal for which the Church universal needs to repent.

Yet though we need to make corporate repentance for our part in it, we also need to recognise how the basic seeds of disunity were planted by the Reformers themselves. In the pursuit of doctrinal purity, they birthed Protestantism into a divided heritage. A notable example was the debate between

Luther and Zwingli over the Eucharist. What began in a mutual desire to deal with the Roman doctrine of transubstantiation, soon became a cacophony of argument, and ended in outright strife. At stake was the question of how Christ was present in the sacraments of bread and wine. Luther emphasised the "This is ..." in the words of institution, whilst Zwingli stressed the "Do this ..." For Zwingli, it was simply about a memorial, that enabled a remembrance. His view was that Luther was lapsing back into Romanism. Luther viewed Zwingli as an enthusiastic fanatic. The exchanges became increasingly ferocious, leading to the time when Zwingli wrote to Luther:

"We make our inference thus: you affirm that the flesh is eaten; we deny it. Therefore, one or other must be wrong."

For once, Luther agreed with his adversary: "One side must be the devil, and God's enemy. There is no middle ground."

Those involved in counselling will know how generational sin has amazing capacity to multiply, often originating a long way back from a relatively definable beginning. Sadly, despite all we owe to the Reformers, this controversy and others were the seed of the disunity that has so hamstrung the church in subsequent generations.

Our disunity is so deep-rooted that the extensive attempts at ecumenism have resulted in only the most modest of achievements. Certainly in recent years much has happened that looks like a step in the right direction. But, relative to its effect on the church's witness to a lost world, much of it amounts to little more than taking the heads off weeds. Indeed the depth of the problem is exemplified by the degree of disunity in the World Council of Churches, based in Geneva. For the past fifty years it has sought to provide a platform for ecumenical dialogue on a broad range of issues.

Yet though it has had its achievements, it is mainly characterised by contentiousness. Its centralist approach, seeking to hold together competing visions and differing convictions, does not suggest that the visible unity of the worldwide church is something that can be planned into being. As an organisation, it seems to be "sinking under the weight of division, controversy and suspicion" to quote the Archbishop of Canterbury. Evidently, something much more fundamental than an official organisation is needed to establish the type of unity that Jesus had in mind.

One view is that if the future harvest of believers were to grow increasingly high, the fences that have divided the church into so many different fields will become increasingly hard to see. So, it is proposed, the primary activity should be the nurturing of that harvest. It is an encouraging picture, which the likes of both Zwingli and Luther would doubtless have appreciated. But it still does not speak of what is needed to deal with the tap-roots of disunity, that have caused the doctrinal ring fences to come into being in the first place. An alternative proposition for unity in the worldwide church was put by Louis Dallière, a pastor of the French Reformed Church. As far back as 1932, he proposed that effective prayer for unity was inextricably bound up with prayer for the illumination of the Jewish people. His conviction was that it will be the converted Jewish people who will restore to the church its visible unity. What the younger son of the parable has not been able to do, despite all his love for Christ, the older brother will help him to accomplish—we do not know where or how—when, restored to the banquet room of his Father, they will prepare together "a radiant church, without stain or wrikle ... but holy and blameless" (Ephesians 5 v27), that will be presented to the Lord on his return.[5]

Dallière put his finger on the extent of what it would really take to excise the tap-roots of disunity and, furthermore, on the price that the church would need to be willing to pay. For it is one thing to plan local ecumenical activity, which can all be quite friendly, and not too costly. Less easy is the establishment of platforms for the planning of international ecumenism. But it is another thing altogether to respond to the Biblical inferences regarding the type of unity that will impact the world. Listen to these words of Jeremiah:

> "In those days, at that time," declares the Lord, "the people of Israel and the people of Judah together will go in tears to seek the Lord their God. They will ask the way to Zion and turn their faces towards it. They will come and bind themselves to the Lord in an everlasting covenant that will not be forgotten."

(Jeremiah 50 v4,5)

The challenge to the western church of our time is how willing it is to come together in tears of repentance, with a mutual desire to look to Zion. The price of doing so from the core of its being may be very high. But were it to do so, then it might find itself having an impact on the world that it could never have planned. Which would certainly be the material of a new season of reformation.

Illustration 3:
A reformed attitude to suffering

A third area of consideration for what a new season of reformation might involve is suffering. Through the work-ethic released by the sixteenth century Reformation, poverty was eliminated in the western world for the average person. In itself, this was a great mercy, for there is no virtue in poverty per se. Yet as physical comfort has increased, the willingness to suffer has decreased, and at that level the western church has been weakened as a result. Even Jesus "learned obedience from what he suffered" (Hebrews 5 v8). But as the western church came to serve both Christ and materialism, it succumbed to the disobedience that bondage to self-indulgence brings. This arises from the subtle entanglement of its underlying value system. One illustration of its effect is the shift of emphasis from *sanctity* of life as a determining value, to *quality* of life. Apparently the worth of life is still being affirmed, yet the focus has shifted dramatically. It has gone from that which calls forth the highest responsibility, to that which is about the maximising of personal benefit. By imbibing such thinking, the mind-set of the western church has been greatly hampered in its understanding of the new attitude to suffering that God might want to call it to.

Clearly, there is great mystery in suffering. It was manifestly not part of God's original created order, and we are also told that there will be no more suffering in the new heaven and the new earth (Revelation 21 v4). Yet during the 'in-between time' the problem of suffering does not go away. At one level, we can simply rationalise it as the consequence for those who have turned their back on God. The suffering of the apparently innocent is however less easy to explain. Then comes the tougher question still of why the God we know to be all-loving and all-powerful permits even those who are the most deeply committed to Him to suffer. Moreover, why He actually calls them into suffering. Take for example the words of commission He gave to Jeremiah personally:

> "Get yourself ready! Stand up and say to them whatever I command you. Do not be terrified by them, or I will terrify you before them. Today I have made you a fortified city, an iron pillar and a bronze wall to stand against the whole land—against the kings of Judah, its officials, its priests and the people of the land. They will

fight against you but will not overcome you, for I am with you and will rescue you," declares the Lord.

(Jeremiah 1 v17-19)

The outworking of this calling was to be immensely costly for Jeremiah, as he found out what it meant in practice to be hated for speaking out God's word. His experiences included being beaten and put in the stocks (ch 20 v2) as well as social rejection and derision (ch 20 v7). He was constantly persecuted by those whose welfare he cherished the most, even to the extent of receiving death threats from the priests and the people (ch 26 v8). On another occasion, he was again beaten and this time imprisoned in a vaulted cell in a dungeon, where he remained a long time (ch 37 v15-16). On yet another, having been accused of sedition, he was lowered into a cistern that had no water in it, and allowed to sink down into the mud to die (ch 38 v6-13). This he only survived because of a rescue involving thirty men, who used ropes, rags and worn-out clothes to hoist him out of the death trap he had been dropped into.

Tradition also has it that Jeremiah is one of those referred to in Hebrews 11 v37 that eventually met his death by being sawn in two. Apparently it happened when, against his will, Jeremiah was taken down into Egypt. There he was placed in a hollow log, which was sawn through. Whether or not that is completely accurate, the fact is that he still endured intense suffering that was not just physical, but also psychological. For Jeremiah was as much flesh and blood as you and I.

Almost his entire lifetime was spent in ministry, beginning "as a child" (ch 1v6), and almost all of it was utterly rejected at the time. What God called him to was his personal experience of mission impossible. His task was to recall a people who were already tottering into national and spiritual catastrophe and all he seemed to get for his faithfulness to God was everything from discouragement, to anguish of body, soul and spirit. He knew that there would be a return from exile after seventy years, but he did not live to see it. Not surprisingly, this was his outburst at God:

> …think of how I suffer reproach for your sake.
>
> (Jeremiah 15v15)

Indeed, he went much further still to utter one of the greatest cries of desolation to be found in the whole of scripture:

> Cursed be the day I was born! May the day my mother bore me not be blessed! Cursed be the man who brought my father the news, who made him very glad saying, "A child is born to you—a son!" May that man be like the towns the Lord overthrew without pity. May he hear wailing in the morning, a battle cry at noon. For he did not kill me in the womb, with my mother as my grave, her womb enlarged for ever. Why did I ever come out of the womb to see trouble and sorrow and to end my days in shame?
>
> (Jeremiah 20 v14-18)

Such was the degree of extremity to which God permitted Jeremiah to go as he spoke out the word of God. It was an experience most of the Reformers encountered as well. Yet it has always been the suffering church, rather than the comfort-zone church, that has known God's power to speak and to act prophetically. The story of the church in China is testimony to this. In 1953, it is estimated that it was comprised of around one million born-again Christians. As persecution spread, the western missionaries were expelled from the country. Today, after almost fifty years of heavy persecution, there are reckoned to be towards one hundred million born again Christians in China. And in South Korea, after centuries of persecution, it is estimated that around half the population are now born again. Indeed the scattering of the early church into Judea and Samaria, described in Acts 8 v1, which happened only because of a great persecution in

Jerusalem, led to the fulfilment of Jesus' promise in Acts 1 v8. This was for a witness that would expand out of Jerusalem, to Judea and Samaria, and ultimately to the ends of the earth.

Despite the mystery of it, the fact is that wherever Christians face costly suffering for the sake of Christ, the gospel is likely to advance, and vice-versa. Because when the church favours self-indulgence rather than suffering, the gospel rarely advances far. For though there is much that we all need to keep receiving about what it means to be dearly loved children (Ephesians 5 v 1), this does not normally lead us to the front lines of spiritual battle. Scripture uses other imagery to encourage us to do this. We are called to be not only "workers" (Matthew 9 v 38), but also "soldiers" (2 Timothy 2 v3) and even "slaves of Christ" (Ephesians 6 v6). Now if our underlying precept is quality of life, we may well interpret such pictures rather more figuratively than literally. As we will Jesus' words about becoming like the grain of seed, that must fall to the ground and die, in order that it may produce many seeds (John 12 v24). It is only when confronted with suffering and persecution for the sake of Christ that such scriptures truly take on the perspective they were intended to have. Only then is the power discovered which, against all rational logic, enables the real witness of God's people to grow in both quantity and quality.

Given the prevailing tolerance of western society, we may consider that persecution for our faith is not very probable in our time frame. It is however not impossible. For if a further season of reformation were to lead the western church into a new attitude toward the Jewish people, then it could happen. Peter Abelard, the twelfth century theologian, said that

To believe that the fortitude of the Jews in suffering would be unrewarded would be to declare that God is cruel. For no nation has ever suffered so much for God.

To discover first hand what anti-Semitism actually tastes like would certainly shift the western church out of its comfort zone. It would require a considerable willingness to move out of its compromise with self-indulgence, and pay a price it does not need to. But were it to do so, it would doubtless discover the blessing that God puts on the witness of a church that chooses to face suffering rather than avoid it.

Inevitably, these three illustrations are speculative, because no one can be sure what the price of a new season of reformation may be. But this much is sure: to suffer for the sake of reformation will be a far preferable alternative than to suffer from the decimation of the western church.

Chapter Ten

The Purpose of More Reformation

THE SIXTEENTH CENTURY REFORMATION was one of those historical events which demonstrates that no one is fully alive until they have something to die for. High price, if not the highest, will be paid when people can see a sufficiently high purpose. It was this that enabled the Reformation to spread like wild-fire amongst the common people. When they found out that the line they had been fed about Christianity was not the truth, they could see a high purpose which warranted a high response. For now they knew that purgatory was not in scripture. That metanoia meant repentance rather than penance, and that justification was by faith rather than by works. So justice and righteousness could be expressed in the every day things of life, and glory could be given to God in the whole of life. Here was rediscovered purpose that it was worth trading just about everything for.

All of which suggests that a new season of reformation would need an equivalent rediscovery of new purpose. Because without it, to relinquish the established structures of the church, let alone our apparent right to comfort-zone Christian living, could look far too costly. Which, as we have already considered, may be why God is withholding the revival that has been felt for so long to be just around the corner. It is to prompt, if not provoke, His people in Britain, Europe and the West to look beyond the immediate benefits of a short-term boost to the life of our church and to consider not only what His greater purpose may be for it, but also what the cost may be.

Now if it was sufficiently recognised that the only other alternative might be the decimation of our church, this would presumably lead to a certain motivation to pay a price. But at best it would be negatively based. Positive motivation would need to be born out of a renewed revelation of the purpose of reformation. Which is not primarily for God to bail out either the church or mankind, however desperate the need of both may be. To think so is to reflect the mentality of the Enlightenment which puts man at the centre of all things, and that sees God's actions as being defined by our needs. Reformation puts God at the centre of all things. It focuses first and foremost on Him, and not on the needs of mankind or on the church. It is about a renewing of the revelation of His glory. Inevitably this has to be outworked within the story of mankind, but the mainspring of reformation is the revelation of God's glory, rather than the resolution of man's needs. Unless understanding of this over-riding principle is widely achieved, today's western church will not be available for what God may at this time want to do so radically within it, let alone through it.

To appreciate what this means for our present times involves us in going back not just to the Beginning, but even to that time before the Beginning. Because Genesis 1 v1 declares that before the beginning of time, God existed. Which means that not only is He over and beyond time, but also that He did not need creation, as we understand it, in order to have meaningful and purposeful existence. It was His sovereign choice to bring creation into existence, and to give it the destiny of His choice. The sum total of all the purpose that mankind ever has or ever will have is therefore subordinate to the purpose of God. God already existed as a fulfillled community, even before He chose to create mankind saying "Let us make man in *our* image" (Genesis 1 v26). God's decision to make mankind as the pinnacle of His creation was therefore to reflect Himself in us. Not because He needed to, but simply because He delighted to. So mankind was to bear God's character, and the world that was given to him was designed that this might be possible, should he wish to use it for this purpose. One commentator puts it this way:

> Creation left to itself is incomplete, and humans are called to be co-creators with God, bringing forth the potentialities the Creator has hidden. Creation is full of secrets waiting to be discovered, riddles which human intelligence is expected to unlock. The world did not spring from the hand of God as wealthy as humans might make it.[1]

What God assigned to mankind was the task of living out heaven on earth through his relationship with every aspect of the world that had been given to him. He was to reflect the image of God in his relationship with himself, as well as with his fellow man. Also in his relationship with the whole of the created order, with all the work of secondary creativity, with the acquisition and use of knowledge, and with the understanding of time and history. It was an extensive realm of opportunity that God gave to mankind, in which to discover and celebrate the real meaning of worship. Everything that has ever happened in the world since then is set within the dealings of God with mankind as he responded to, or rebelled against, this calling.

The contrast of this overview compared with the secular view of mankind cannot be over-stated. For it limits the understanding of man's identity and purpose to that which evolves out of the statement "In the beginning, nature…" Man may be the highest form of evolution, but that is all. Nothing more. There is no eternal perspective for mankind, because we are simply here as consumers, and our self-centred goal is to maximise the available resources for our greatest benefit. But with more and more of us, each consuming more and more, life in this view looks like no more than an exercise in futility. It is simply about surviving for as long as we can, and as best as we can, before the whole thing runs out. Which when reduced to its basics, leads to an exceedingly hollow view of man. Let alone when compared with the Biblical account that calls mankind to bring about an earth that will be "full of the knowledge of the Lord as the waters cover the sea" (Isaiah 11 v9).

The Bible's description of man is that he is God's vice-regent, called to bring about the comprehensive development of a world in harmony not only with itself, but even with the One who is already a trinity in community, and who has no need of external relationship in order to exist. Man's purpose was therefore to be a worshipper. He was to bring glory to God throughout the whole of His life on earth, and to enjoy the blessing of God as he worshipped in this way. Everything God gave mankind in the resources of the created order were therefore to be considered as the materials of worship. Working with those materials was to involve process, but that process was not to be the end in itself.

Beyond the process of life was to be the purpose of life, which was the giving of glory to God. Everything in life, right through to the most menial deed, was intended to be about worship that honoured the God who was at the centre of all things. No aspect of life was to be exempt and in so far as that was done, God would place blessing on mankind.

The end purpose of reformation is therefore neither the alleviation of the sufferings of a society rooted in secularism, nor the revitalising of a church that is in dramatic decline. However desperate the need of both may be, this is still only process. From our viewpoint, that process may warrant all the attention it can get, but the ultimate purpose of that process is not centred on mankind. Mankind is not at the centre of all things. It is God alone who is there, and the purpose of reformation is to restore that truth, and give glory to Him as it does so. Which cannot be fully done within the four walls of a church or a conference, but only through the whole of life and the entire network of relationships it involves. Reformation is therefore about the recovery of true worship, being that which glorifies God throughout every sinew of every society. Indeed this is what Revelation 14 v6-7 defines as the "eternal gospel," the goal of which is about far more than the salvation of individual souls. The eternal gospel given there to the angel to proclaim to those who live on the earth, to every nation, tribe, language and people, was articulated as this:

> Fear God and give Him glory, because the hour of His judgement has come. Worship Him who made the heavens, the earth, the sea and the springs of water.

Here is the statement of what all history is moving toward under the sovereign hand of God, whatever twists and turns mankind might add along the way. Its consummation will not be that humankind has somehow made it through to the end of all things earthly. It will not even be in the celebration of the personal salvation of the faithful. Though God desires that all should come to repentance, even this is secondary to His stated end-time purpose towards which all history is moving inexorably - one incomprehensibly gigantic act of worship, in which every creature in heaven and on earth and under the earth and on the sea, and all that is in them, is to sing:

> To Him who sits upon the throne and to the Lamb be praise and honour and glory and power, for ever and ever!
>
> (Revelation 5 v13).

Into nothing less than this context—that preceded the Beginning as we understand it, and will extend beyond the End as we understand it—must be set the purpose of Reformation. Which is to lift humanity's eyes off our compulsive preoccupation with ourselves and our circumstances up to the greatness of the reason behind our creation, and to the ultimate destiny of all history.

The Centrality of Worship

Some however struggle with such a notion of worship. C.S.Lewis certainly did. As a young Christian he wrote in these terms:

> When I first began to draw near to belief in God and even for some time after it had been given to me, I found a stumbling block in the demand so clamorously made by all religious people that we should 'praise' God; still more in the suggestion that God Himself demanded it. We all despise the man who demands continued assurance of his own virtue, intelligence or delightfulness; we despise still more the crowd of people round every dictator, every millionaire, every celebrity, who gratify that demand. Thus a picture, at once ludicrous and

horrible, both of God and of His worshippers, threatened to appear in my mind. The Psalms were especially troublesome to me in this way—'Praise the Lord,' 'O praise the Lord with me,' and 'Praise Him'... It was hideously like saying, 'What I most want is to be told I am good and great.' And mere quantity of praise seemed to count; 'Seven times a day do I praise thee' (119:164). It was extremely distressing. It made one think what one least wanted to think. Gratitude to God, reverence to Him, obedience to Him, I thought I could understand; not this perpetual eulogy. Nor were matters mended by a modern author who talked of God's 'right' to be praised.

The breakthrough came for Lewis when he understood what actually happened in worship.

I did not see that it is in the process of being worshipped that God communicates His presence to men. .... Even in Judaism the essence of the sacrifice was not really that men gave bulls and goats to God, but that by their so doing God gave Himself to men.[2]

Lewis had fathomed the reason why God had given the people of Israel rules for every aspect of life. Rules that were not given to oppress them, but to remind them constantly of the centrality of His glory. For when God said "I am the Lord your God ... you shall have no other gods before me" (Exodus 20 v2-3) He meant it. He went on to say "I, the Lord your God, am a jealous God" (v5). So from business dealings and principles for farming through to the intimacy of their marital relationships, the worship of God was to be central. They were to be, by the whole of their lifestyle, a distinctive people, a treasured possession, a kingdom of priests and a holy nation (Exodus 19 v5-6). They were to stand out from all other people as a people who worshipped Almighty God, in spirit, and in truth, that blessed Him, and who enjoyed distinctive blessing in consequence. They were in effect to be the embodiment of reformation that would point other nations to the one true God. Indeed, that through them, the nations of the world would themselves find blessing, as God had promised to Abraham (Genesis 12 v3).

The calling of the people of Israel was to demonstrate the reversal of what had happened at the Fall. When, through the misdirection of worship that took place there, man lost the capacity to be both natural and supernatural. Instead he became just plain unnatural. For that is what sin originally resulted in and still does. Sin is the attempt to draw life from something other than what God has ordained, by giving worship to it. This was the battle of Eden. For God had created all men and women to need some form of spiritual life to feed off in order to live spiritually. It was to be drawn from whom, or from what, they worshipped. It was to be their deepest means of sustenance. Satan had no power to change the way God had created mankind to function. It was one of those incontrovertible laws God had built in to the created order. So Satan could not stop a single man, woman or child, from being a worshipper. The only thing he could do was to tempt mankind to alter the direction of his worship. From his viewpoint, it didn't matter what to. Anything would do, as long as it wasn't the one, true God that was being worshipped. Then Satan knew that deformation would result, and the image of God would be marred in mankind. The temptation worked, and mankind became idolatrous, which in God's sight was to be spiritually adulterous, for the boundary of fidelity had been broken. Mankind therefore became separated from the glory of God, of which even the slightest glimpse was then to be overwhelming. From this point, mankind fell short of the glory of God and the further short of it he fell, the less he realised what he was falling short of.

In His mercy, God spelt out to the people of Israel what true worship should look like, in a detailed, step by step guide that applied to every area of life. One of the most graphic pictures of the central place of worship was given in the instructions for setting encampments in the wilderness. Numbers chapters 2 and 3 give extensive instructions for how three tribes should camp to the north of the tabernacle, three to the east, three to the west, and three to the south. In the middle of the encampment was to stand the tabernacle, symbolising how everything should centre on the worship of God. So both by symbol and instruction, Israel was given the opportunity to restore its worship to the way it was originally meant to be and at the same time to rediscover the greatness of the purpose for which God had created the human race.

> Worship is the submission of all our nature to God. It is the quickening of the conscience by His holiness; the nourishment of the mind with His truth; the purifying of the imagination by His beauty; the opening of the heart to His love; the surrender of will to His purpose—and all this gathered up in adoration, the most selfless emotion of which our nature is capable and therefore the chief remedy for that self-centredness which is original sin and the source of all sin.

In these words Archbishop William Temple summarised the rediscovery of that purpose through worship, and this indeed was the essence of the worship God wanted Israel to offer. Yet Israel's subsequent history tells the sad story of its failure to worship God with a genuine heart. For the heart of their problem was the problem of their heart. It was so fundamentally 'deceitful' (Jeremiah 17 v9) that Jeremiah had to extend warning after warning about the judgement that comes upon false worship. And not just to those who were overtly worshipping idols, but even to those who went to the house of the Lord to worship.

> This is what the Lord says: "Stand in the courtyard of
> the Lord's house and speak to all the people of the towns
> of Judah who come to worship in the house of the Lord.
> Tell them everything I command you; do not omit a
> word. Perhaps they will listen and each will turn from
> his evil way. Then I will relent and not bring on them
> the disaster I was planning because of the evil they have
> done."
>
> (Jeremiah 26 v2-3)

It was not the superficial appearance of their worship that
was the problem. They were worshipping as they had been
instructed to. The problem was in what lay beneath the
surface of their worship. For all they were really interested
in was self-serving religion. They worshipped God purely
and simply for what they got out of it. They still needed,
according to Jeremiah (ch7 v3), to reform their ways and
their actions.

Jeremiah had no difficulty in speaking out the judgement
of God on the specific sins of the people. But this was not
his main target. Severe as this was, he was not so concerned
about the details of the process of sin that they were
entangled in, as the fact that they had lost sight of the high
purpose to which they had been called. They were to be a
people who demonstrated the blessing that came on those
who trusted in the Lord for every aspect of life, as distinct
from those who turned their back on Him:

> This is what the Lord says: "Cursed is the one who trusts
> in man, who depends on flesh for his strength and whose
> heart turns away from the Lord. He will be like a bush
> in the wastelands; he will not see prosperity when it
> comes. He will dwell in the parched places of the desert,
> in a salt land where no-one lives. But blessed is the man
> who trusts in the Lord, whose confidence is in Him. He
> will be like a tree planted by the water that sends out its
> roots by the stream. It does not fear when heat comes;

its leaves are always green. It has no worries in a year of drought and never fails to bear fruit."

(Jeremiah 17 v5-8)

The people of Israel were meant to be a living example to the nations of the fact that if God were honoured in every aspect of life, then He would put blessing on their lives. There was be a degree of reciprocity as man recognised his responsibility to work out in practice what it meant to be the image-bearer of God. Choice and discipline were called for and would result in distinctive blessing. This was the abiding principle in God's economy according to which mankind was to live in this world. As the Westminster Confession memorably captured it over two thousand years later, the answer to the question of the chief end of man is not just "to glorify God…" but also "… to enjoy Him for ever." It is not dutiful subservience but evident enjoyment that God intends for humanity as we live out the calling we were created for. God's intention was that Israel's expression of this was to be so winsome that nations would come to them, recognising the falseness of their own gods, and seeking out who was the true Lord:

> …the nations will come from the ends of the earth and say, "Our fathers possessed nothing but false gods, worthless idols that did them no good. Do men make their own gods? Yes, but they are not gods!" Therefore I will teach them—this time I will teach them my power and my might. Then they will know that my name is the Lord.
>
> (Jeremiah 16 v19-21)

It grieved God deeply that Israel had no real understanding of the greatness of purpose to which He had called them. He grieved for Israel because, as they lost their sense of purpose, they lost both their identity and their potential to find succour in the enjoyment of knowing God. It was a vicious circle that God longed for Israel to break out of, both for their own sake and for the sake of the nations He desired to bless through them. Nor was this a mild longing; for in the prophetic picture God gave to Jeremiah of the wineskins that He would smash (ch.13 v12-14) and the jar He told Jeremiah to smash (ch.19 v1-15) was the revelation of how severe was the judgement of God, because the people of Israel were "stiff-necked and would not listen" (ch.17 v23).

From His perspective, it was not an optional extra to have a people who would declare what it meant to reflect His glory through the whole of their lives, and the whole of their nation.

Saved for Worship

We can only surmise about the extent to which Jeremiah foresaw the coming of the Messiah who, in His grace, would enable people to do what they were otherwise unable to, which is to offer true worship to God. Clearly he had some notion of the possibility of One who would come to save both individuals and nations. This was his confidence:

> Heal me, O Lord, and I shall be healed; save me and I shall be saved, for you are the one I praise.
>
> (Jeremiah 17 v14)

He also prophesied about a future salvation in these terms:

> "The days are coming," declares the Lord, "when I will fulfill the gracious promise I made to the house of Israel and to the house of Judah. In those days and at that time I will make a righteous Branch sprout from David's line; he will do what is just and right in the land. In those days Judah will be saved and Jerusalem will live in safety. This is the name by which it will be called: The Lord Our Righteousness."
>
> (Jeremiah 33 v14-16)

However limited Jeremiah's understanding of who that future king would be, or what exactly would be the nature of His kingship, the coming of Jesus fulfilled both his hopes and his prophecy. For Jesus Christ inaugurated a kingdom that would know no end. It was a kingdom that would express God's reign and rule on earth. Not just to bring righteousness to the hearts of individual believers, but to every sphere of life. The salvation He came to bring was not merely to rescue people out of the world and guarantee them a safe journey to heaven, like a divine search and rescue mission. He came to redeem the whole created order. All things were to be brought back into conformity with the standards of a just and holy God. Which is why the very first petition Jesus taught the disciples to pray was "Your kingdom come, your will be done on earth as it is in heaven" (Matthew 6 v10). Heaven was to be lived out on earth. This was where the disciples' intercession was to start.

Jesus' final commission was "make disciples of all nations ... teaching them to obey everything I have commanded you" (Matthew 28 v19-20). The way He topped and tailed His instructions made it clear what their principle work was to be. It was not to be the winning of souls throughout the nations of the world, but to disciple the nations themselves, that they would become righteous. In other words, through the restoration of individuals into right relationship with God all the secondary relationships of man would also be restored. The very structures of societies were to be impacted by the gospel, saved and discipled. Culture itself was to be redeemed. For in this was the essence of true worship, which is the giving of glory to God in every sphere of life, from the greatest to the least.

It was for the saving of all creation that Jesus Christ had come into the world, because God so loved the whole world. The real impact of God's gift of His one and only Son is contained in the Greek word used in John 3 v16 for 'world'—*kosmos*—meaning everything there is in the created order. To have said 'humanity' here would have been far weaker. God's willingness to pay the price of redemption was therefore for each and every part of it, that it might all be brought back into the harmony He had originally created it to enjoy. Which explains why Jesus said that the good news was to be preached to "all creation" (Mark 16 v15). As Paul theologised it, God's intention through Jesus Christ was to "reconcile to himself *all* things, whether things on earth or things in heaven" (Colossians 1 v20). Also that "the creation waits in eager expectation for the sons of God to be revealed" so that it will be "liberated from its bondage to decay and brought into the glorious freedom of the children of God" (Romans 8 v19 & 21). The redemption Jesus came to bring was therefore not just for the healing of the primary relation of mankind with God, but equally for the healing of all of creation's secondary inter-relationships. Because until salvation impacts each of these areas of life, the true basis for worship that man was principally created to express has not been restored. For it is not just with instruments of string and wind that God called man to produce the music of worship, but with every instrument of the created order.

The notion that the plan of salvation is principally for our personal benefit is commonplace. It fits so easily into the consumerist and individualist spirit of our age, that centres on the meeting of our personal needs. If that is our presupposition, it will fundamentally affect our interpretation of scripture. Such as how we understand God's purpose in giving His one and only Son, that whoever believes in Him "shall not perish, but have eternal life." It can simply centre on what God did for me at Calvary. But though we should still be eternally grateful for this, it may lead to a self-serving religion, that is a worship which is actually no better than that which Jeremiah had to confront in his day.

Those who have a personal experience of salvation through Jesus Christ would generally consider themselves far removed from the hypocrisy of Jeremiah's day, and from the judgement that goes with false worship. Yet the problem with spiritual blindness, as with physical blindness, is that it is very hard to tell where you are actually standing. Which is why the very limited effectiveness of the western church of today should surely prompt us to consider whether there is amongst us a spiritual blindness, as there was in Jeremiah's day. A blindness that prevents us from discerning the superficiality of our worship in all those areas of life in which God intended true worship to be expressed. Caused quite simply through being mesmerised by the modern-day idols of ambition, comfort and success.

The greatest reason that God saved us was that we might not perish in the sense of losing what we were created to be. Which is what the nation of Israel was called to be, but failed to be—utterly committed worshippers of God who reflect His glory to a world that has misdirected its worship. For that to happen, salvation cannot be not something to be kept purely for personal consumption. It is not even just for sharing with other individuals. Salvation is also for all those secondary relationships that suffered collateral damage when man's primary relationship with God was destroyed by sin. Yet without such a vision of all things being before God as *coram Deo*, then the true vision of worship God created mankind for has yet to be recovered. Herein is the real purpose of reformation.

The phrase 'gnostic evangelicalism' has been used to describe the type of Christianity that gives testimony to the experience of personal salvation, but makes no extension of that salvation to the structures of the world around. [3] As such it reflects the separation in Greek thinking of the sacred from the secular. Gnosticism, derived from the Greek word *gnosis* meaning knowledge, is a term describing systems of belief that claimed to impart special knowledge of God. In particular of His relation to the world, and to men, and of redemption. The possession of such knowledge was supposed to enlighten the initiated and guarantee the salvation of their souls. [4] Gnostic evangelicalism is a residue of the thinking of the Enlightenment, that took the rationalism of the Greeks as one of its basic tenets. Indeed, that made it so non-negotiable that all else had to be filtered through it.

A most graphic picture of this is expressed in the architecture of the Cathedral of St. Pierre, in the old city of Geneva. It was from here that Calvin preached daily, fuelling the sixteenth century Reformation as it spread across Europe. Though still open through the week for prayer, it is mostly tourists who nowadays enter the Cathedral through the neo-classical Greek main doorway, with its triangular roof shape supported on pillars. This was not the main doorway of Calvin's time, but a new façade added in 1756. The original had fallen into decay, and it was decided that a piece of architecture should be used for the new entrance that would express the spirit of the age. Thus it was that the entrance to the very place from where the Reformation message was proclaimed was designed in the style of a Greek temple.

Physically, the new doorway was simply a later addition that came between the pulpit from which Calvin used to preach and the world outside. But spiritually, it represents the impact of the Enlightenment on the message of the Reformation. For it depicts the division introduced between the sacred and the secular, which the Enlightenment drew from rational, Greek thought. That doorway is therefore a parable etched in stone that speaks of what has to be first passed through to get back to the original message of the

Reformation and then passed back through if it is to be taken out into the modern-day world. Many of those who do so may be unaware, like the tourists, that this Greek 'doorway' is a later addition, very different from the original. It is therefore most appropriate that in the corner of the courtyard in front of the Cathedral of St. Pierre, hiding almost out of sight, is a statue of Jeremiah. He is weeping, almost unable to look at the Cathedral, reflecting the comment of his real life counterpart:

> But if you do not listen, I will weep in secret because of your pride; my eyes will weep bitterly, overflowing with tears, because the Lord's flock will be taken captive.
>
> (Jeremiah 13 v17)

However unintentionally gnostic evangelicalism is imbibed, it has immense consequences for the mission of the church. For it leads to a private and pietistic Christianity, rather than a public and incarnational Christianity. It centres on Jesus as Lord of my heart, rather than "if not Lord of all, then He is not Lord at all." It centres on saving souls for heaven, rather than making disciples of all nations and it looks to the return of Christ as being about freedom from this present suffering, rather than the culmination of the process of reconciliation.

All of which leads to the most fundamental separation of outlook, between those who in effect operate out of a theology of waiting, and those who operate out of a theology of action. Those who wait may well be doing much to bring others to come and wait with them until the Lord returns and singing the Lord's praises while they wait. But this is a very different understanding of worship from that which looks to see how the ground can be won back from Satan, in the multitude of ways he seeks to deceive the nations. Otherwise, if only by default, the glory in this world apparently goes to him. His motto, mistaken as it is, could well be "if we don't lose, we win."

Although the kingdom of God is both now and not yet, the worship we are called to is the heralding of the not yet into the now. Sometimes it will be purely symbolic, as was the encampment of the twelve tribes of Israel around the tabernacle, three on each side, prefiguring the Holy City, the new Jerusalem (Revelation 21 v10-14). At other times however, it will be a literal and physical expression of the end-time victory of the kingdom of God in the present. For if the glory and the honour of the nations is to be brought into the new Jerusalem, and the leaves of the tree of life are to be for the healing of the nations (Revelation 21 v26 & 22 v2), there should be a foretaste of that in the here and now. A foretaste revealed by tangible evidence of the healing of that which has wounded nations and deformed their potential to manifest the glory and honour of God.

Such a vision may seem beyond reach, given the complexity of what controls modern society. However, it is no more impossible today than on that day when Jesus gave the Great Commission to a bewildered group of eleven disciples. Yet this was to lead to the official conversion of the Roman empire within three centuries, and subsequently across church history to many amazing stories of what God has done through individual men and women to touch the lives of nations; the sixteenth century Reformation is just one of those stories.

At the last day there will be the comprehensive destruction of the "shroud that enfolds all peoples, the sheet that covers all nations" (Isaiah 25 v7). Then the all-enveloping deception that Satan has put not just on individuals, but on whole groups of people, will be removed. Then every lie and counterfeit will be exposed, and there will be no more blindness to the absolute truth. But even ahead of that time, God's people have been given the power of His Spirit to "declare the praises of Him who has called you out of darkness into His wonderful light"(1 Peter 2 v9). Not just praises regarding what He has done for us personally, but because of His power to heal nations. Which means for our part, to seek such openings as we can find to express the distinctive justice and righteousness of God, that speaks of His kingship. A formidable task indeed, but not an impossible one. To quote the words Martin Luther wrote in his hymn of 1529 known as *A safe stronghold:*

> And let the prince of ill
> Look grim as e'er he will,
> He harms us not a whit;
> For why? his doom is writ;
> A word shall quickly slay him.

A fundamental expression of worship is therefore the slaying of Satan's power in every area of life by the offensive action of God's people. For spiritual warfare is not just about withstanding Satan's advances. Much more critically, it is about taking the ground back off him and filling it with the glory of God. This requires a greater understanding of Christian living than results from gnostic evangelicalism alone. It needs a living rediscovery of what is truly at the heart of the gospel, which goes far beyond a salvation that simply gets otherwise lost souls into heaven. It is that righteousness and justice may, through the grace of our Lord Jesus Christ, be expressed in the whole of life. This is the demonstration that God's will is being done throughout the earth, as it is throughout heaven. It was the possibility of this that was rediscovered in the sixteenth century and it is this same possibility which needs to be discovered afresh if there is to be a new season of reformation.

Chapter Eleven

The Possibility of More Reformation

THE CHURCH IN BRITAIN, EUROPE AND THE WEST may perhaps be reaching its most critical point in half a millennium. Though it has not happened suddenly, the realisation that there may now be only two alternatives, reformation or decimation, underscores the urgency of the situation that has been reached.

What began in the great high of the sixteenth century Reformation, impacting not just the church, but through it the nations of the western world, left a legacy that shapes them to this day. Yet the western church, and indeed the society in which it is set, is the recipient of other legacies as well. For the effect of the Enlightenment that followed the Reformation not only quenched belief but also reduced its legacy to legalism. It put man at the centre of all things, displacing the Christian gospel to the fringes of relevance in what was redefined as the 'real' world. In an attempt to remain plausible, the church compromised the gospel, as it imbibed the rationalism that was at the heart of the spirit of the age. When modernism then emerged out of the Enlightenment, much of the membership of the western church found itself unable to resist the secular pull. For it had become captive to its surrounding culture that had split the sacred from the secular. So the church was subverted from its calling. No longer did it understand the gospel as that which enables God's will to be done on earth as it is in heaven, and for the nations to be discipled. Instead it became fenced into the personal salvation of individuals. This meant that however enthusiastic believers might become, or however large their church, the gospel largely remained as a private matter for their spare time. Such that whenever renewal began in individuals, it most often stopped where it started. It rarely led on to seeing the whole of life as *coram Deo*, as being lived before God.

As it lost its grip on this basic principle of the Reformation, the western church increasingly slid down the slippery slope into nominalism. The result was the reverse of what the early church saw, as it grew from a minority into a majority, and finally with the conversion of the Roman empire, into a monopoly. The more inconsequential the church became, the less motivation there was for its members to lay down their lives for the gospel. Hence its decline which has only accelerated as the twentieth century has progressed. For as it became increasingly acquiescent to the values of a secularised culture, and to the indulgence of materialism, it was rendered ever more impotent to be as salt in a tasteless world and light in a dark world. Meanwhile, the broader spiritual scene has begun to move from modernism into post-modernism and the New Age. But whilst the western world opens itself to that which is mystical, much of the established church remains stuck a long way back up the trail from where the action is now happening.

Yet despite the seriousness of the situation, the way this has happened has been rather more subtle than sudden. Writing as long ago as the nineteen sixties, Francis Schaeffer commented that nowhere in history has there been so great a turning from the knowledge of God in such a short span of time as had recently been witnessed in northern European culture, as well as that of America and Canada.[1] It had been a turning away not just from the truth of the Reformation, but from the culture built upon that truth, including the balance of freedom and form it brought in both state and society. A balance never known anywhere in the world before. He commented that had a questionnaire been distributed in New York in the nineteen twenties, one would have found that though many people may not have been Christians, they would at least have had a clear idea what Christianity was about. Trafalgar Square around 1890 would have been the same. But that if the same thing had been done at the time he was writing in the nineteen sixties, most would have little or no concept of the true essence of Christianity. For the Christian consensus had been lost. If that was true then, how much more must it be true as the twenty-first century begins.

It can be debated whether the demise of Europe has been because of the virtual collapse of the church within it, or vice-versa. Yet either way the culpability of the western church cannot be evaded. For it scarcely seems to have noticed what has happened. Or if it has, it does not appear to be overly concerned. Nonetheless, we can be sure that God has never ceased to watch the responses of His people to the changing of circumstances, or care about them. For He is an unchanging God. Right at the start of Jeremiah's ministry, God gave him a picture that was to form his future thinking:

> The word of the Lord came to me: "What do you see, Jeremiah?" "I see the branch of an almond tree" I replied.
>
> The Lord said to me, "You have seen correctly, for I am watching to see that my word is fulfilled."
>
> (Jeremiah 1 v11-12)

Though God was playing with the Hebrew words for watching *(soqed)* and almond tree *(saqed)*, He was not playing with His own words. It was the realisation of this that caused Jeremiah to become known as the 'weeping prophet' (ch.9 v10). For the more he spoke out God's words of warning, the deeper it grieved him to see how blithely indifferent were the people of God. Jeremiah knew that God would permit judgement to come upon His people if they did not take notice and that he would simply lift His protection off His people, in the way that He warned would happen:

> I will forsake my house, abandon my inheritance; I will give the one I love into the hands of her enemies. My inheritance has become to me like a lion in the forest. She roars at me; therefore I hate her. Has not my inheritance become to me like a speckled bird of prey that other birds of prey surround and attack? Go and gather all the wild beasts; bring them to devour. Many shepherds will ruin my vineyard and trample down my field; they will turn my pleasant field into a desolate wasteland. It will be made a wasteland, parched and desolate before me; the whole land will be laid waste because there is no-one who cares. Over all the barren heights in the desert destroyers will swarm, for the sword of the Lord will devour from one end of the land to the other; no-one will be safe. They will sow wheat, but reap thorns; they will wear themselves out but gain nothing. So bear the shame of your harvest because of the Lord's fierce anger.
>
> (Jeremiah 12 v7-13)

However, perhaps because of its remarkable history, the western church seems to think it has a freehold on God's blessing and protection. So it continues in its dreams, but it may well be doing so at its peril. For it should not forget that the God it claims to serve is the same God who slayed Uzzah for daring to touch the ark of His covenant, but then permitted the ark to fall into enemy hands when it was treated as a talisman. He is the same God who allowed the Temple He had designed so precisely to later be reduced to rubble once it was abused. If the western church reckons its future is guaranteed simply because of its past, it is deluding itself. To think so is to depend on the same type of false assurance that Jeremiah recognised God had appointed him to warn against:

> Then the Lord reached out His hand and touched my mouth and said to me, "Now, I have put my words in your mouth. See, today I appoint you over nations and kingdoms to uproot and to tear down, to destroy and to overthrow, to build and to plant."
>
> (Jeremiah 1 v9&10)

Jeremiah's ministry sprang from the knowledge that God never ceases to observe His people and that when they turn from Him, He will first warn them repeatedly. But that if they will not heed His warnings, there will eventually come a time when He will bring them to a watershed. From which point things have to go one way or the other. Intervening to revive what is left from the past, that it may go on as it did before, ceases to be an option. A far more radical solution is the only alternative, involving His people either being uprooted and overthrown, or upbuilt and newly planted. Which means that the conjunctions of circumstance that point to a possible new season of reformation for the western church might also point to the other outcome being equally near. For if reformation is a real possibility, so too may be decimation.

Given the decline of the western church that has been going on for so long, the relevance of the warning God gave through Jeremiah should not be lost sight of. For the church in other parts of the world is now sufficiently strong for God to work out His purposes through them. Whereas at the turn of the century, over eighty percent of the world's Christians were white and living in the northern hemisphere, it is now far less than fifty percent. How ever much God may desire to use the church in Europe as He did in the past, that through it the nations might again hear His word, He is not obliged to do so - either in principle or in practice. Indeed for the sake of His holy name, lest it be considered synonymous with a decadent generation of His people, it is not impossible that God could instead permit significant judgement to come upon it. Especially if it persistently deludes itself about its state before Him. For this is how God spoke to the people of Judah:

"Will you steal and murder, commit adultery and perjury, burn incense to Baal and follow other gods you have not known, and then come and stand before me in this house which bears my Name, and say "We are safe"—safe to do all these detestable things? Has this house, which bears my Name, become a den of robbers to you? But I have been watching!" declares the Lord.

(Jeremiah 7 v9-11)

Though it is evident that God has not yet entirely rejected the present generation of the western church, there is still no basis for complacency. In fact, it may be a grave risk to assume that it is any more safe than the people of Judah that Jeremiah prophesied to. For, if the western church simply carries on into the twenty-first century as it finished the twentieth century, then the even greater severity of these words might come true for the next generation:

> When you tell them all this, they will not listen to you; when you call to them, they will not answer. Therefore say to them, "This is the nation that has not obeyed the Lord its God or responded to correction. Truth has perished; it has vanished from their lips. Cut off your hair and throw it away; take up a lament on the barren heights, for the Lord has rejected and abandoned this generation that is under His wrath."
>
> (Jeremiah 7 v27-29)

Profound responsibility may therefore lie with our present generation, that where we need to respond to correction, we do so. Not just in order for an extensive decimation of the western church in the next generation to be avoided, though that should be reason enough. But to do so with the positive prospect of the other outcome, which is a new season of historic reformation. That the church might be upbuilt, and the process of secularisation reversed, such that nations may be discipled by the church as they were five centuries ago. The words of Jeremiah are therefore as apposite today as when he first spoke them:

> You of this generation, consider the word of the Lord.
>
> (Jeremiah 2 v31)

The legacy of the generations

Certainly the western church of today is not just a product of its own actions. The reality is that it is to a large extent the product of what has gone on in previous generations. It still enjoys a residual blessing from the sixteenth century Reformation, and from many other good things which have happened since then. But it is also deeply impoverished by the compromise that has long been made with the spirit of the age. Yet whatever the mixed legacy of the previous generations, the responsibility rests with the present generation for what we do with it. For in the hands of our generation lies the determination of the legacy that will be passed to the next generation. Now is the day of their salvation, and should it even only be a possibility that the most critical moment of the last five hundred years is fast being approached, then this is a most serious responsibility indeed.

If we, like the people of Judah, remain blithely indifferent then it is we who will have to carry the accountability for what the next generation will find itself bearing. Because, as God made it clear to Jeremiah, there is a remarkable capacity for sinfulness to be passed from one generation to another:

"Therefore I bring charges against you again," declares the Lord. "And I will bring charges against your children's children."

(Jeremiah 2 v9)

However unfair this might seem, the connection of the generations was something Jeremiah plainly believed to lie within the sovereignty of God, for this was how he prayed:

Ah, Sovereign Lord, you have made the heavens and the earth by your great power and outstretched arm. Nothing is too hard for you. You show love to thousands, but bring the punishment for the fathers' sins into the laps of their children after them. O great and powerful God, whose name is the Lord Almighty, great are your purposes and mighty are your deeds.

(Jeremiah 32 v17-19)

It may seem inconsistent that a loving God, whose purposes are so great and for whom nothing is too hard, can permit the transmission of blame for sin from one generation to another. But in that same mechanism exists the key to the potential of reformation, not only to heal curse from generations past, but to also minister blessing to generations in the future. For it was in the greatness of God's purpose that what happens in one generation should affect what happens in the next. Because seen from the perspective of before the Fall, it was a plan for good and not for evil that the legacy of the generations should be such an intrinsic part of life. In Genesis 1 v11-28, we are told that when God called forth vegetation, its on-going existence depended on it bearing seed. Plants and trees were to bear seed in their fruit, according to their kinds and this God saw as good. When God created fish and birds, they were also commanded to be fruitful and to increase, again according to their kind. So it was with livestock and creatures that moved along the ground. Each subsequent generation was to be the reproduction of the previous generation.

However, in the creation of mankind, God took this principle yet further still, to reproduce His own image. Part of that image is to pass on blessing to others freely. So God made man to convey the blessing of one generation on to another. As a result of this we are blessed beyond our comprehension. We cannot begin to imagine what sort of a world it would be if each generation had to re-invent the wheel. Let alone how we would manage without all the infra-structure that previous generations have passed on to us. We depend for example on the buildings, roads and bridges that others constructed by the sweat of their brow. We harness the technology they struggled to develop. We are enriched by their labours with art and music, literature and education. Also, for Christians there is the heritage left by the saints who have gone before, in many forms such as books and hymns, traditions as well as translations of scripture. If all we had was that which the present generation has produced, life would not just be shallow, it would perhaps even be unliveable.

Yet because of the Fall, the very principle God intended for greatest blessing became also the channel of greatest curse and the process of redemption has not changed that stark reality. Like the law of gravity, the generational principle was an unalterable law of the created order. It was not like the law in Leviticus with all its do's and don'ts that could be superseded by grace. Instead, grace has to be worked out within the context of what is unavoidably handed down to us from previous generations. Some of which is blessing, and some of which is not. Hence the phrase Jeremiah used to describe the effect of generational sin:

> The fathers have eaten sour grapes, and the children's teeth are set on edge.
>
> (Jeremiah 31 v29)

Jeremiah looked to the time when that would no longer be true, but until then he knew what the reality was. The sinful actions of one generation had great propensity to cause curse to come upon the next generation and even to be multiplied within it. For the seed of the next generation is in the fruit of the previous generation, with effect to the third and the fourth, and in certain cases even to the tenth generation (Deuteronomy 23 v2). Which is why another dose of revival, in the sense it is traditionally understood, is an all too inadequate prescription for the western church if the suggested diagnosis of its condition is correct. It doesn't just need a bit of revitalising, it needs to be fundamentally reformed. Because there is no other way it can be severed from the curse which has come from previous generations, that has played its part in bringing the church to its present point. Apart, that is, from experiencing a process of uprooting and tearing down, destruction and over-throwing.

The other side of the coin, however, is that if curse can so evidently be passed from one generation to another, how much more can blessing also be passed on. The seed of blessing for another generation is equally in the fruit produced in the present generation. Which is why the significance of this present generation of the western church should be recognised, not only in the context of generations past, but also of generations future. For with the aid of the God for whom nothing is too hard, and whose purpose is that man might be restored to His image, the reformation of the church within one generation is possible. The past can be cut off, and the future can be blessed. Always keep in mind what happened within Luther's generation as he declared, "Here I stand," or in Geneva within one generation as Calvin sought to build a model of the 'City of God'. Indeed not only within that generation, but from that generation, to the third and fourth generations and in some cases, as far as the tenth. If it happened once, then it can surely happen again. In this is both the challenge and the responsibility the western church faces as it begins its third millennium. To bear fruit that carries the seed of Reformation for the next generation.

The Generation of Reformation

Despite the bleak outlook that Jeremiah faced, God nonetheless interwove his prophecy with great words of encouragement about what would still lie ahead. At the start of it, God spoke to him about the scope that still existed for building and planting (ch.1v9-10). Then at the end of it, like this:

> "In those days, at that time" declares the Lord, "the people of Israel and the people of Judah together will go in tears to seek the Lord their God. They will ask the way to Zion and turn their faces towards it. They will come and bind themselves to the Lord in an everlasting covenant that will not be forgotten."
>
> (Jeremiah 50 v4-5)

At the centre of the book are five enthralling chapters that speak of the everlasting love of the Lord. There will come a time, God said, when:

> "They will be my people, and I will be their God. I will give them singleness of heart and action, so that they will always fear me for their own good, and the good of their children after them.

> "As I have brought all this great calamity on this people, so I will give them all the prosperity I have promised them. Once more fields will be bought in this land of which you say, "It is a desolate waste, without men or animals, for it has been handed over to the Babylonians." Fields will be bought for silver, and deeds will be signed, sealed and witnessed in the territory of Benjamin, in the villages around Jerusalem, in the towns of Judah and in the towns of the hill country, of the western foothills and of the Negev, because I will restore their fortunes," declares the Lord.
>
> (Jeremiah 32 v38-39 & v42-44)

God left Jeremiah in no doubt that, if necessary, He would first allow great calamity to fall upon His people, should they leave Him with no other option. But beyond any such calamity, was a promise of restoration. For His over-arching purpose was that they would be brought to a point where they would again truly fear Him, and have concern not only for themselves but for a future generation. Which was why God called Jeremiah to do something very practical, to express his confidence in that promise. It was to go out and buy a field. Jeremiah 32 v8-14 recounts the story of how he weighed out seventeen shekels of silver in order to make the purchase. Terms and conditions were set out, and the deeds were signed and sealed. But Jeremiah gave instruction that one copy of the deeds should be placed in a clay jar, enabling them to be preserved for a very long time. He was well aware that if the city was first handed over to the Babylonians, many years might go by before the prophesied restoration took place.

Though it may be far from inevitable that God will permit an equivalent calamity to fall upon the western church, should it not change course of its own volition, the possibility cannot for ever be excluded. For He is the same God who spoke to Jeremiah in these terms:

> I have made you a tester of metals and my people the ore, that you may observe and test their ways. They are all hardened rebels, going about to slander. They are bronze and iron; they all all act corruptly. The bellows blow fiercely to burn away the lead with fire, but the refining goes on in vain; the wicked are not purged out. They are called rejected silver, because the Lord has rejected them.
>
> (Jeremiah 6 v27-30)

Even the remotest possibility of such a rejection should challenge us deeply. For it is a terrible scenario, yet one which cannot be absolutely ruled out. Beyond it, we may be sure that God would look to a time of restoration, though it may only be distant. Futhermore that He would also call His prophets to actions that, ahead of time, would speak of a western church no longer subverted, but which again had singleness of heart and action. Yet what it might mean before that time of restoration is outside our comprehension. Which is why we may be sure that God will do all He can to divert the western church into the direction of reformation. But the outcome will depend on our recognition of the reality of what may lie ahead, as well as of what needs to happen within the western church if it is to find the way of reformation.

This will be no small thing, because such things are not easily admitted and the longer such admission is delayed, the more calamitous the situation becomes. Such was the lesson the Swiss watch industry learnt the hard way a few years ago.

In between 1979 and 1982, employment dropped from sixty-five thousand to fifteen thousand, due entirely to the arrival of the quartz watch.[2] Though it had even been invented in Switzerland, the industry preferred to hang on to its traditional use of tiny gears and springs to record the passing of time. This led first to a decline that no amount of effort to revive the industry could reverse. Then almost to collapse. Pride centred on past success had first to be relinquished, before admission could be made of the need for the most fundamental of change. Had it done so sooner, it could have spared itself not only much pain, but also much lost opportunity.

Even as a secular illustration, the story of the Swiss watch industry has great relevance to the western church of today. However, the battle that the church is engaged in is not primarily commercial but spiritual, and this complicates the interpretation of what is going on yet further. Because in Satan's strategy, it may suit him better that the western church be sustained in its nominalism. For a tamed animal is much less dangerous than a wounded animal that is suddenly woken up. Hence the problem of the western church being far more with subtle, luring attractions than with sudden, lunging attacks. Satan's aim is to keep it from realising what it has become blind to and bound by. Let alone what it needs to be doing for the blessing of a future generation. So he works at keeping it preoccupied with secondary issues that prevent it from seeing the greater perspective, knowing that the church cannot give what it doesn't have.

Against this, however, is the evidence of both scripture and history, that God can reveal to His people the truth of what is happening, even when they can't see it for themselves. As He promised to Jeremiah in one of his times of confinement, when he was unable to find out what was going on. This was God's word to him:

> This is what the Lord says, He who made the earth, the
> Lord who formed it and established it—the Lord is His
> name: "Call to me and I will answer you and tell you
> great and unsearchable things that you do not know."
>
> (Jeremiah 33 v2-3)

Evidently Jeremiah relentlessly called out to God for such revelation, judging by the great and unsearchable things he was given to prophesy. In the same way Luther, as he grappled with the question of righteousness, rediscovered not only the gospel but also what precisely should be tackled in the established church of his day, even to the extent of how he should go about it. Likewise, God showed Calvin, through an exceedingly tenacious struggle, how reformation could be put into practice in every day life, as the story of Geneva bears out.

Such testimony should surely encourage a belief that God would want to give a similar revelation which is equally relevant to today's situation, and yet which from our perspective cannot otherwise be discerned. That He would want to speak of how the gospel might be rediscovered in our time in terms extending far beyond the notion of personal salvation, to deeply challenge a church that presently takes its faith on and off like a sweater. To enable it to rediscover both the fear of a holy God, as well as a worship that over-arches the whole of life. To release it from being locked into things rational, institutional and traditional, in order to be principally defined by those things which incarnate the kingdom of God. For it will be nothing less than this which will sear the hearts of the nations, let alone confront them with what it means for every aspect of life to centre on the glory of the one true God.

Living near a Swiss lakeside, there are times when we enjoy the most glorious views of the mountains. But often in autumn and winter all we see is cloud. The reason being that

Alpine clouds have a remarkable ability to get stuck in the valleys that contain the lakes. Yet take the little train up the mountain above us, and you may well break into brilliant sunshine, with panoramic views of the mountain tops. On such days, down in the valley that contains the lake, there may well be a big fluffy cloud. So is it a cloudy day or a sunny day? It all depends whether you're up above or down below.

Unfortunately much of the western church is spiritually down below, under a cloud, and groping around. But God's heart is surely to raise it up once more to the heights of reformation. Because the cloud hasn't overcome the sun, and the darkness hasn't overcome the light even if, from down below, it feels like it. Secularism, relativism, post-modernism, and every other 'ism' all put together are still not greater than the gospel of Jesus Christ. It is for the rediscovered revelation of this that God wants us to relentlessly call out to Him from our position down below that we might see it from His perspective up above.

At the start, I invited you to join with me in thinking about how the great Reformers would define the agenda of our times, if not the opportunity of it. I also suggested that my own reflections could only be one very small part of the process that is needed. Which is why I would like to encourage you to become actively involved in it. To do so imagine that 'www' stands not for the World Wide Web, but for Wittenburg, Worms and Wartburg, the three places where Luther made the statements that were to have such worldwide consequences. Imagine then that you are a modern-day Luther, looking for an equivalent debate on the state of the western church. So what would you post on the 21st Century Reformation Website?

Whether or not you choose to energize the debate this way (which you really can do—see below for details!) there remains a choice which you cannot avoid. If only by default, you will choose whether or not you believe God may be saying again to this generation of the western church what He said to the people of Judah:

> See, I am setting before you the way of life and the way of death.

(Jeremiah 21 v8)

Most of the sixteenth century Reformers are best described as reluctant heroes. But there was something they had each realised that motivated them to be relentless in their pursuit of reformation. They knew that on the choices they and their generation made hinged what would happen in the generations of the future. They looked beyond the immediate to the need to provide both the seed and the field of Reformation, in order that there could be a living harvest in the future.

What followed were indeed great and unsearchable things, that achieved far more even in their next generation than they ever thought or imagined. The way of life was found not just for individuals, or even for the church as a whole, but for the nations. Had they not recognised what they did, it would have been a very different story, not only for their next generation, but even for ours.

Much courage will have to be exercised if the western church of today is to break out of the captivity that Jeremiah, or any or the sixteenth century Reformers, would diagnose it as being in. Let alone to return to take its stand, declaring it can do no other. Yet as it possibly faces its most critical cross-roads of the last five hundred years, the prophecy of Jeremiah about what may otherwise come next should be heeded. Both clergy and laity need to take note of what history has written on the road signs and guideposts along the highway it has travelled (ch.31 v21), and to make some brave choices in the light of that.

Or else the weeping of Jeremiah may once more have been in vain.

Soli Deo Gloria.

The 21st Century Reformation Discussion Group on the Internet

To post your own 95 theses (or maybe just one or two!), to declare where you or the church needs to stand, or to post any other piece, point your newsreader to <u>alt.soc.reformation</u>.

Your newsgroup reader is probably bundled with your browser (in *Internet Explorer* it is under 'Tools'); it enables you to follow and contribute to any discussion threads you may find there.

Notes

Chapter 1

1   Alister E. McGrath, *A Life of John Calvin* (Oxford, Blackwell 1990) p.95

2   Timothy George, *Theology of the Reformers* (Nashville, Broadman 1988) p.180

3   Francis Higman, *Why the Reformation?* (Université de Genève 1996) p.10

Chapter 2

1   Rundle Charles, *Chronicles of the Schönberg-Cotta Family* (London, Thomas Nelson) p.169

2   J.H. Merle D'Aubigné, *History of the Reformation of the Sixteenth Century* (Religious Tract Society, London, 1846) p.70

3   ibid. p.245

Chapter 3

1   Ed. Alister McGrath, *Modern Christian Thought* (Oxford, Blackwell 1993) p.152

2   Richard Lovelace, *Dynamics of Spiritual Life* (Illinois, InterVarsity Press 1979) p.417

3   Os Guiness, *The Gravedigger File* (London, Hodder & Stoughton 1983) p.51

4   Andrew Walker, *Telling the Story* (London, SPCK 1996) p.51

5   Michael Green, *I Believe in Satan's Downfall* (London, Hodder & Stoughton1981) p.47

Chapter 4

1   Lesslie Newbigin, *The Gospel in a Pluralist Society* (London, SPCK 1989) p.213

2   Graham Cray, *From Here to Where?* (London, Board of Mission Occasional Paper No 3, 1992)

3   Margaret Brearley, *The New Age Movement* (Skepsis Supplement of Anglicans for Renewal, Summer 1994) quoting Hannah Arendt "The Origins of Totalitarianism"

4   Andrew Walker, *Telling the Story* (London, SPCK 1996) p.187

Chapter 5

1   J. Tracy, *The Great Awakening. A History of the Revival of Religion in the Time of Edwards and Whitefield.* (Edinburgh, The Banner of Truth Trust, 1997) p.216

2   E.Evans, *The Welsh Revival of 1904,* (Evangelical Press of Wales,1969) quoted in Rob Warner, Prepare for Revival (London, Hodder and Stoughton, 1995) p.43

3   Jessie Penn-Lewis, *The Awakening in Wales,* Overcomer, quoted in H.H.Osborn, Revival, God's Spotlight (Godalming, Highland, 1996) p.104

4   Owen Murphy, quoted in Mark Stibbe, *Revival* (Crowborough, Monarch, 1998) p.31

5   Jonathan Edwards, *The Surprising Work of God* (New Kensington, PA 1997) p.115f.

6   Ibid., p.70

7   Mark Stibbe, *Revival* (Crowborough, Monarch, 1998) pp.29-31

8   Clifford Longley, *The Daily Telegraph* September 25th 1998

Chapter 6

1   Howard Snyder, *Liberating the Church* (Marshall, Basingstoke 1983) p.28

2   Charles Colson, *The Body* (Word Publishing, Dallas, 1992) p.240

3   Joseph Alleine, *Alarm to the Unconverted* (Banner of Truth 1967) pp.93-94

Chapter 7

1   *Time Magazine* April 13th, 1998

2   Walter J. Chantry, *Today's Gospel, Authentic or Synthetic?* (Banner of Truth 1970) p.45

3   Darrow Miller, *With all your Mind* (Monograph of Food for the Hungry, 1993, available from 7729 E. Greenway Rd., Scottsdale, AZ 85260)

4   J. Gresham Machen, quoted in J.I.Packer's *Fundamentalism and the Word of God* (IVF, London 1958) pp.35-36

Chapter 8

1   Charles Colson, *The Body* (Word Publishing, Dallas,1992) p.32

2   John Stott, *Issues Facing Christians Today* (Marshall Pickering, London 1984) p.6 quoting David O. Mowberg, The Great Reversal (Lippincott Philadelphia 1972)

3   Roland Bainton, *Here I Stand: A Life of Martin Luther* (Abingdon-Cokesbury New York 1950) p.50

4   George Grant, *Bringing in the Sheaves* (Wolgemuth & Hyatt, Brentwood TN 1988) pp55-6, quoted by John Wimber, Equipping the Saints, 4th quarter 1995

Chapter 9

1   George H. Stevens, *Strife between Brothers* (Olive Press, London, 1979) p.34

2   Max I. Dimont, *The Indestructible Jews* (Signet, New York, 1973) p.284

3   David Bogosian, US Centre for World Mission

4   David Barrett, *World Christian Encyclopaedia* (Oxford University Press, 1982)

5   Peter Hocken, *The Glory and the Shame* (Eagle, Guildford, 1994) p.93

Chapter 10

1   Michael Novak, *The Spirit of Democratic Capitalism,* (New York, Simon & Schuster, 1982) p.39

2   C.S.Lewis, *Reflections on the Psalms,* (London, Fontana, 1964) pp.77-79

3   Darrow Miller, *The Kingdom of God and the Discipling of Nations,* (Mono